Contents

Nonfiction Reading Practice Is Important

Research indicates that more than 80 percent of what people read and write is nonfiction text. Newspapers, magazines, directions on new products, application forms, and how-to manuals are just some of the types of nonfiction reading material we encounter on a daily basis. As students move through the grades, an increasing amount of time is spent reading expository text for subjects such as science and social studies. Most reading comprehension sections on state and national tests are nonfiction.

Each Unit Has...

A Teacher Resource Page

Vocabulary words for all three levels are given. The vocabulary lists include proper nouns and content-specific words, as well as other challenging words.

A Visual Aid

The visual aid represents the topic for the unit. It is intended to build interest in the topic. Reproduce the visual on an overhead transparency or photocopy it for each student.

Articles at Three Reading Levels

Each unit presents three articles on the same topic. The articles progress in difficulty from easiest (Level 1) to hardest (Level 3). An icon indicates the level of the article—Level 1 (▪), Level 2 (▪▪), Level 3 (▪▪▪). Each article contains new vocabulary and ideas to incorporate into classroom discussion. The Level 1 article gives readers a core vocabulary and a basic understanding of the topic. More challenging vocabulary words are used as the level of the article increases. Interesting details also change or increase in the Levels 2 and 3 articles.

Level 1

Level 2

Level 3

Readability

All of the articles in this series have been edited for readability. Readability formulas, which are mathematical calculations, are considered to be one way of predicting reading ease. The Flesch-Kincaid and Fry Graph formulas were used to check for readability. These formulas count and factor in three variables: the number of words, syllables, and sentences in a passage to determine the reading level. When appropriate, proper nouns and content-specific terms were discounted in determining readability levels for the articles in this book.

Nonfiction Reading Practice, Grade 2 • EMC 3313 • ©2003 by Evan-Moor Corp.

Student Comprehension Pages

A vocabulary/comprehension page follows each article. There are five multiple-choice questions that provide practice with the types of questions that are generally used on standardized reading tests. The bonus question is intended to elicit higher-level thinking skills.

Level 1

Level 2

Level 3

Additional Resources

Six graphic organizers to extend comprehension are also included in the book. (See page 4 for suggestions for use.)

Famous Person

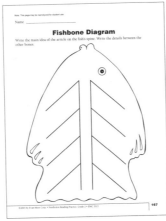

Fishbone Diagram

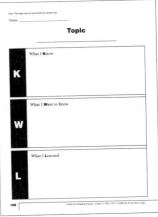

KWL Chart

Sequence Chart

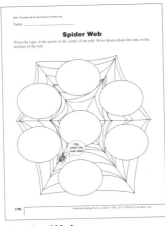

Spider Web

Word Quilt

How to Use *Nonfiction Reading Practice*

Planning Guided Reading Instruction

The units in this book do not need to be taught in sequential order. Choose the units that align with your curriculum or with student interests.

- For whole-group instruction, introduce the unit to the total class. Provide each student with an article at the appropriate reading level. Guide students as they read the articles. You may want to have students read with partners. Then conduct a class discussion to share the different information learned.

- For small-group instruction, choose an article at the appropriate reading level for each group. The group reads the article with teacher guidance and discusses the information presented.

- The articles may also be used to assist readers in moving from less difficult to more challenging reading material. After building vocabulary and familiarity with the topic at the appropriate level, students may be able to successfully read the article at the next level of difficulty.

Presenting a Unit

1. Before reading the articles, make an overhead transparency of the visual aid or reproduce it for individual student use. Use the visual to engage student interest in the topic, present vocabulary, and build background that will aid in comprehension. This step is especially important for visual learners.

2. Present vocabulary that may be difficult to decode or understand. A list of suggested vocabulary words for each article is given on the teacher resource page. Where possible, connect these words to the visual aid.

3. Present and model several appropriate reading strategies that aid in comprehension of the expository text. You may wish to make an overhead transparency of the reading strategies checklist on page 5 or reproduce it for students to refer to as they read.

4. You may want to use one of the graphic organizers provided on pages 166–171. Make an overhead transparency, copy the organizer onto the board or chart paper, or reproduce it for students. Record information learned to help students process and organize the information.

5. Depending on the ability levels of the students, the comprehension/vocabulary pages may be completed as a group or as independent practice. It is always advantageous to share and discuss answers as a group so that students correct misconceptions. An answer key is provided at the back of this book.

Nonfiction Reading Practice, Grade 2 • EMC 3313 • ©2003 by Evan-Moor Corp.

Name _____

Reading Checklist

Directions: Check off the reading hints that you use to understand the story.

Before I Read

_____ I think about what I already know.

_____ I think about what I want to learn.

_____ I predict what is going to happen.

_____ I read the title for clues.

_____ I look at the pictures for clues.

While I Read

_____ I stop and retell to check what I remember.

_____ I reread parts that are confusing.

_____ I read the captions under the pictures.

_____ I make pictures of the story in my mind.

_____ I figure out ways to understand hard words.

After I Read

_____ I think about what I have just read.

_____ I speak, draw, and write about what I read.

_____ I reread favorite parts.

_____ I reread to find details.

_____ I look back at the story to find answers to questions.

The Statue of Liberty

Introducing the Topic

1. Reproduce page 7 for individual students, or make a transparency to use with a group or your whole class.

2. Present the diagram of the statue to the students. Read the caption and labels to connect the new vocabulary with a graphic representation.

Reading the Selections

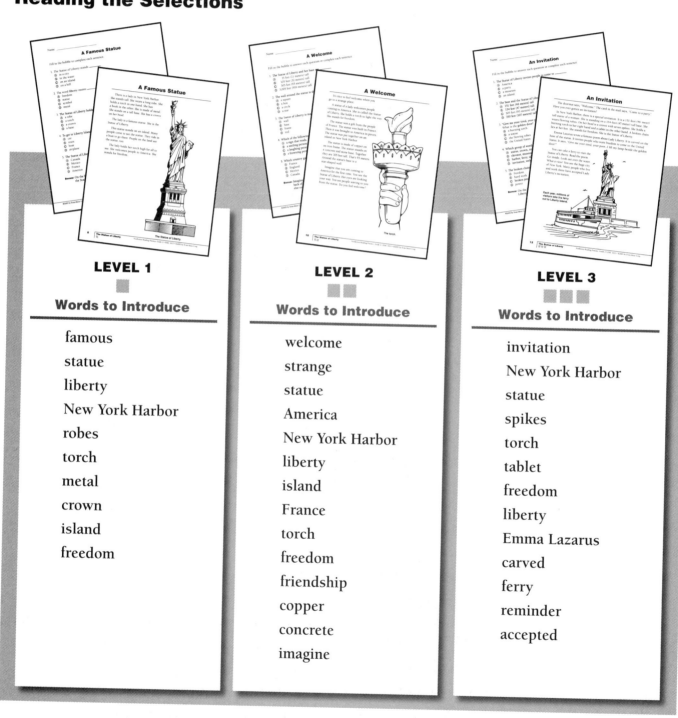

LEVEL 1

Words to Introduce

famous

statue

liberty

New York Harbor

robes

torch

metal

crown

island

freedom

LEVEL 2

Words to Introduce

welcome

strange

statue

America

New York Harbor

liberty

island

France

torch

freedom

friendship

copper

concrete

imagine

LEVEL 3

Words to Introduce

invitation

New York Harbor

statue

spikes

torch

tablet

freedom

liberty

Emma Lazarus

carved

ferry

reminder

accepted

Nonfiction Reading Practice, Grade 2 • EMC 3313 • ©2003 by Evan-Moor Corp.

The Statue of Liberty

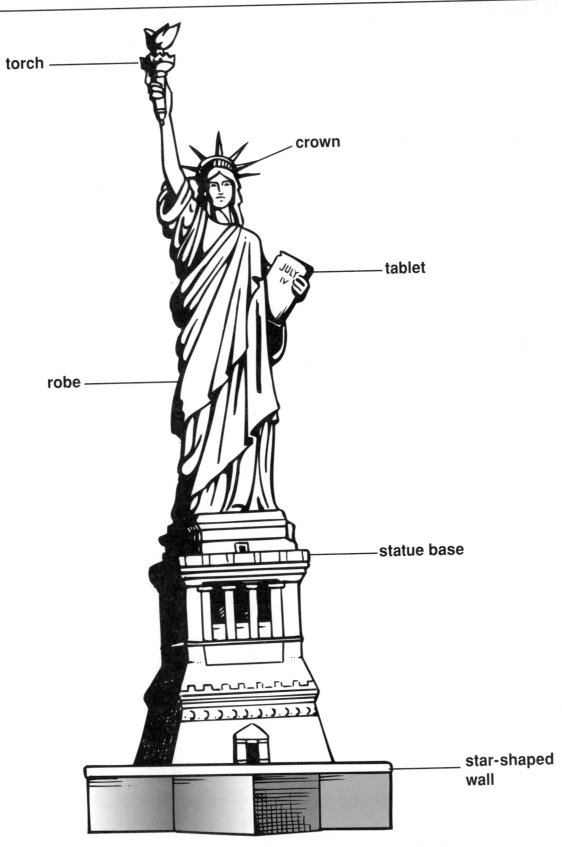

torch

crown

tablet

robe

statue base

star-shaped wall

The Statue of Liberty stands on an island in New York Harbor.

A Famous Statue

There is a lady in New York Harbor. She stands tall. She wears a long robe. She holds a torch in one hand. She has a book in the other. She is made of metal. She stands on a tall base. She has a crown on her head.

The lady is a famous statue. She is the Statue of Liberty.

This statue stands on an island. Many people come to see the statue. They ride in a boat to go there. People on the land see the statue, too.

The lady holds her torch high for all to see. She welcomes people to America. She stands for freedom.

The Statue of Liberty

Nonfiction Reading Practice, Grade 2 • EMC 3313 • ©2003 by Evan-Moor Corp.

Name _____

A Famous Statue

Fill in the bubble to complete each sentence.

1. The Statue of Liberty stands _____.
   - Ⓐ in a city
   - Ⓑ in the water
   - Ⓒ on an island
   - Ⓓ on a hill

2. The word **liberty** means _____.
   - Ⓐ freedom
   - Ⓑ statue
   - Ⓒ symbol
   - Ⓓ metal

3. The Statue of Liberty holds _____.
   - Ⓐ a robe
   - Ⓑ a torch
   - Ⓒ a crown
   - Ⓓ a base

4. To get to Liberty Island, people travel by _____.
   - Ⓐ car
   - Ⓑ train
   - Ⓒ boat
   - Ⓓ airplane

5. The Statue of Liberty welcomes people to _____.
   - Ⓐ Canada
   - Ⓑ Mexico
   - Ⓒ France
   - Ⓓ America

Bonus: On the back of this page, write three things that you learned about the Statue of Liberty.

A Welcome

It's nice to feel welcome when you go to a strange place.

A statue of a lady welcomes people coming to America. She is called the Statue of Liberty. She holds a torch to light the way. She stands for freedom.

The statue was a gift from the people of France. The statue was built in France. Then it was brought to America in pieces. The statue was put together on an island in New York Harbor.

The statue is made of copper on an iron frame. The statue stands on a concrete and stone base. Together they are 305 feet tall. That's 93 meters. Around the statue's base is a star-shaped wall.

Imagine that you are coming to America for the first time. You see the Statue of Liberty. Her eyes are looking your way. You see people waving to you from the statue. Do you feel welcome?

The torch

Nonfiction Reading Practice, Grade 2 • EMC 3313 • ©2003 by Evan-Moor Corp.

Name _____

A Welcome

Fill in the bubble to answer each question or complete each sentence.

1. The Statue of Liberty and her base are _____.
   - Ⓐ   35 feet (11 meters) tall
   - Ⓑ   105 feet (32 meters) tall
   - Ⓒ   305 feet (93 meters) tall
   - Ⓓ 3,005 feet (916 meters) tall

2. The wall around the statue is shaped like _____.
   - Ⓐ a square
   - Ⓑ a box
   - Ⓒ a circle
   - Ⓓ a star

3. The Statue of Liberty is made of copper on an iron _____.
   - Ⓐ wall
   - Ⓑ base
   - Ⓒ frame
   - Ⓓ rod

4. Which words below would make you feel welcome in a new place?
   - Ⓐ a sign that reads, "Members Only"
   - Ⓑ a smiling person saying, "Please come in."
   - Ⓒ a laughing person saying, "I don't care."
   - Ⓓ a frowning person saying, "Go away."

5. Which country gave the Statue of Liberty to America?
   - Ⓐ France
   - Ⓑ England
   - Ⓒ Mexico
   - Ⓓ Canada

Bonus: Imagine that someone is visiting you for the first time. On the back of this page, write words of welcome you could use. What else could you do to welcome the visitor?

An Invitation

The doormat says, "Welcome." The card in the mail says, "Come to a party." Have you ever gotten an invitation?

In New York Harbor, there is a special invitation. It is a 151-foot (46-meter) tall statue of a woman. She is standing on a 154-foot (47-meter) tall base. She wears a flowing robe. On her head is a crown with seven spikes. She holds a burning torch in her right hand and a tablet in the other hand. A broken chain lies at her feet. She stands for freedom. She is the Statue of Liberty.

Emma Lazarus wrote a famous poem about Lady Liberty. It is carved on the base of the statue. It invites people who want freedom to come to the United States. It says, "Give me your tired, your poor...I lift my lamp beside the golden door!"

You can take a ferry to visit the Statue of Liberty. Read the poem. Go inside. Look out over the water. What a view! You see the huge city of New York. Many people who live and work there have accepted Lady Liberty's invitation.

Each year, millions of visitors take the ferry out to Liberty Island.

Nonfiction Reading Practice, Grade 2 • EMC 3313 • ©2003 by Evan-Moor Corp.

An Invitation

Fill in the bubble to answer each question or complete each sentence.

1. The Statue of Liberty invites people to come to _____.
   - Ⓐ America
   - Ⓑ a party
   - Ⓒ a museum
   - Ⓓ an island

2. The base and the Statue of Liberty stand _____.
   - Ⓐ 151 feet (46 meters) tall
   - Ⓑ 154 feet (47 meters) tall
   - Ⓒ 305 feet (93 meters) tall
   - Ⓓ 350 feet (107 meters) tall

3. "Give me your tired, your poor...I lift my lamp beside the golden door."
   What is the **golden door**?
   - Ⓐ a burning torch
   - Ⓑ a statue
   - Ⓒ the flowing robes
   - Ⓓ the United States

4. Which group of words has something to do with water?
   - Ⓐ statue, crown, torch
   - Ⓑ elevator, museum, history
   - Ⓒ harbor, ferry, island
   - Ⓓ invitation, welcome, poem

5. The broken chain is a symbol of _____.
   - Ⓐ freedom
   - Ⓑ hard work
   - Ⓒ broken promises
   - Ⓓ power

Bonus: On the back of this page, write a paragraph that tells how the Statue of
Liberty is like an invitation.

Our President

Introducing the Topic

1. Reproduce page 15 for individual students, or make a transparency to use with a group or your whole class.

2. Present the chart to students. Point out the six major roles of the president and explain what each entails.

Reading the Selections

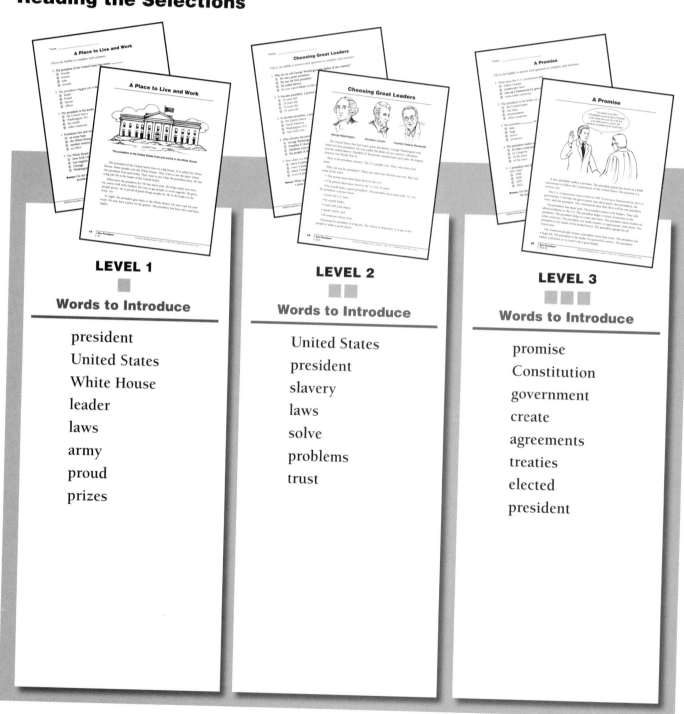

LEVEL 1

Words to Introduce

president

United States

White House

leader

laws

army

proud

prizes

LEVEL 2

Words to Introduce

United States

president

slavery

laws

solve

problems

trust

LEVEL 3

Words to Introduce

promise

Constitution

government

create

agreements

treaties

elected

president

Our President

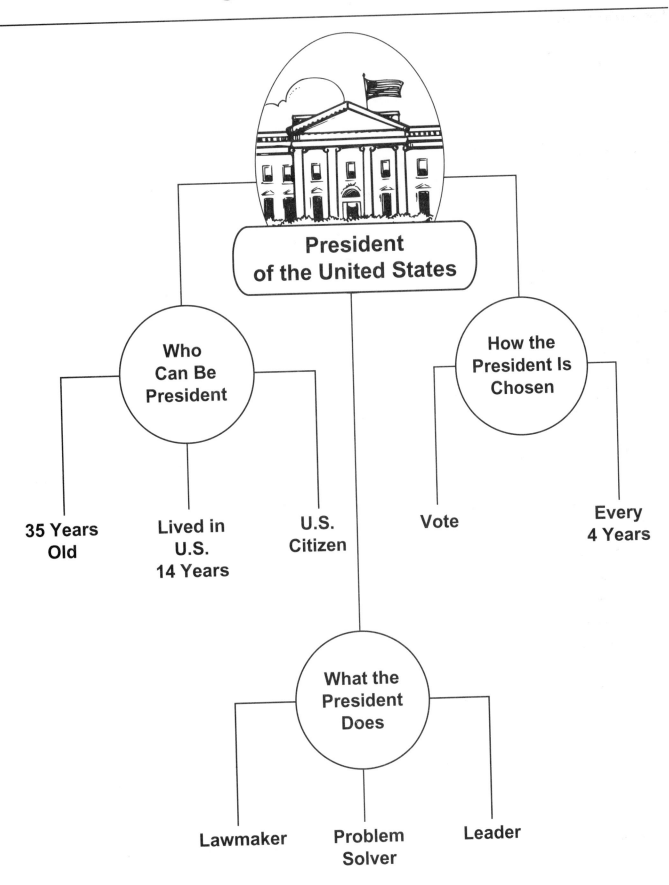

President
of the United States

Who
Can Be
President

How the
President Is
Chosen

35 Years
Old

Lived in
U.S.
14 Years

U.S.
Citizen

Vote

Every
4 Years

What the
President
Does

Lawmaker

Problem
Solver

Leader

A Place to Live and Work

The president of the United States lives and works in the White House.

The president of the United States lives in a big house. It is called the White House. Many people visit the White House. They want to see the place where the president lives and works. They want to see what the president does. He has a big job. He is the leader of the United States.

What does the president do? He has many jobs. He helps make new laws. He meets with other leaders. He tries to get people to work together. He gives people prizes. He is proud of good things people do. He is the leader of the army, too.

At night, the president goes back to the White House. He may read. He may study. He may have a party for his guests. The president has busy days and busy nights.

Nonfiction Reading Practice, Grade 2 • EMC 3313 • ©2003 by Evan-Moor Corp.

Name _____

A Place to Live and Work

Fill in the bubble to complete each sentence.

1. The president of the United States has many _____.
   - Ⓐ friends
   - Ⓑ houses
   - Ⓒ jobs
   - Ⓓ awards

2. The president's biggest job is being a good _____.
   - Ⓐ leader
   - Ⓑ friend
   - Ⓒ lawyer
   - Ⓓ officer

3. The president is the leader of _____.
   - Ⓐ the United States
   - Ⓑ Washington, D.C.
   - Ⓒ the world
   - Ⓓ other countries

4. Presidents live and work in _____.
   - Ⓐ an army base
   - Ⓑ the White House
   - Ⓒ another country
   - Ⓓ an office

5. The White House is in _____.
   - Ⓐ New York City
   - Ⓑ Los Angeles
   - Ⓒ Chicago
   - Ⓓ Washington, D.C.

Bonus: On the back of this page, write two or three sentences that tell about the president's jobs.

©2003 by Evan-Moor Corp. • Nonfiction Reading Practice, Grade 2 • EMC 3313

Choosing Great Leaders

The United States has had many great presidents. George Washington was America's first president. He was called the father of our country. Abraham Lincoln ended slavery. Franklin D. Roosevelt created many new jobs. He helped America win World War II.

How is the president chosen? The U.S. people vote. They vote every four years.

Who can run for president? There are rules that tell who can run. Here are some of the rules:

- The person must have been born in the U.S.

- The person must have lived in the U.S. for 14 years.

- The person must be at least 35 years old.

Who would make a good president? The president does many jobs. To run for president, a person must:

- know the U.S. laws,

- be a good leader,

- work well with others,

- speak clearly, and

- be someone others trust.

Choosing the president is a big job. The choice is important. It is up to the people to make a good choice.

George Washington

Abraham Lincoln

Franklin Delano Roosevelt

Nonfiction Reading Practice, Grade 2 • EMC 3313 • ©2003 by Evan-Moor Corp.

Name _____

Choosing Great Leaders

Fill in the bubble to answer each question or complete each sentence.

1. Why do we call George Washington the **father of our country?**
   - Ⓐ He was a great president.
   - Ⓑ He was the first president.
   - Ⓒ He ended slavery.
   - Ⓓ He was a good father to his children.

2. To become president, a person must be at least _____.
   - Ⓐ 14 years old
   - Ⓑ 25 years old
   - Ⓒ 35 years old
   - Ⓓ 55 years old

3. To become president, a person must have been born in _____.
   - Ⓐ the United States
   - Ⓑ North America
   - Ⓒ Washington, D.C.
   - Ⓓ New York City

4. Who chooses the president?
   - Ⓐ George Washington
   - Ⓑ Franklin D. Roosevelt
   - Ⓒ Abraham Lincoln
   - Ⓓ the people of the U.S.

5. How often is a vote taken?
   - Ⓐ every 3 years
   - Ⓑ every 4 years
   - Ⓒ every 5 years
   - Ⓓ every 6 years

Bonus: What makes a great president? On the back of this page, tell what a great president does.

A Promise

I do solemnly swear that I will faithfully execute the office of President of the United States and will, to the best of my ability, preserve, protect, and defend the Constitution of the United States.

A new president makes a promise. The president places his hand on a Bible and swears to follow the Constitution of the United States. The promise is a serious one.

The U.S. Constitution was written in 1787. It sets up a framework for the U.S. government. It divides the government into three parts: the lawmakers, the court, and the president. The constitution says that there will be one president.

The president has many jobs. The president meets with leaders. They talk about problems in the U.S. The president helps to think of answers to the problems. The president helps to create new laws. The president meets leaders of other countries. The president can make treaties, or agreements, with them. The president is the leader of the armed forces. The president speaks for all Americans.

The American people choose a president every four years. The president has a huge job. The president is the leader of a powerful country. The president makes a promise to try hard to be a good leader.

Nonfiction Reading Practice, Grade 2 • EMC 3313 • ©2003 by Evan-Moor Corp.

Name _____

A Promise

Fill in the bubble to answer each question or complete each sentence.

1. What does the U.S. Constitution do?
   - Ⓐ makes treaties
   - Ⓑ creates new laws
   - Ⓒ sets up a framework for government
   - Ⓓ visits other countries

2. The president is the leader of _____.
   - Ⓐ the United States
   - Ⓑ one state
   - Ⓒ all presidents
   - Ⓓ other countries

3. The president _____ to do his best.
   - Ⓐ asks
   - Ⓑ begs
   - Ⓒ starts
   - Ⓓ promises

4. The president makes agreements, or treaties, with leaders _____.
   - Ⓐ of other countries
   - Ⓑ in Congress
   - Ⓒ of the army
   - Ⓓ of the navy

5. A president was elected in 1996. When was the next presidential election after that?
   - Ⓐ 1998
   - Ⓑ 2000
   - Ⓒ 2001
   - Ⓓ 2002

Bonus: On the back of this page, write a paragraph that tells about the promise the president makes.

©2003 by Evan-Moor Corp. • Nonfiction Reading Practice, Grade 2 • EMC 3313

Harriet Tubman

Introducing the Topic

1. Reproduce page 23 for individual students, or make a transparency to use with a group or your whole class.

2. Present the map to the students. Discuss the issues of slavery in the South and freedom in the North. Point out Harriet Tubman's birthplace of Maryland and her destination of Pennsylvania. Trace her route to freedom, emphasizing that it was a dangerous journey for a slave. Harriet Tubman's trip took almost 15 days.

Reading the Selections

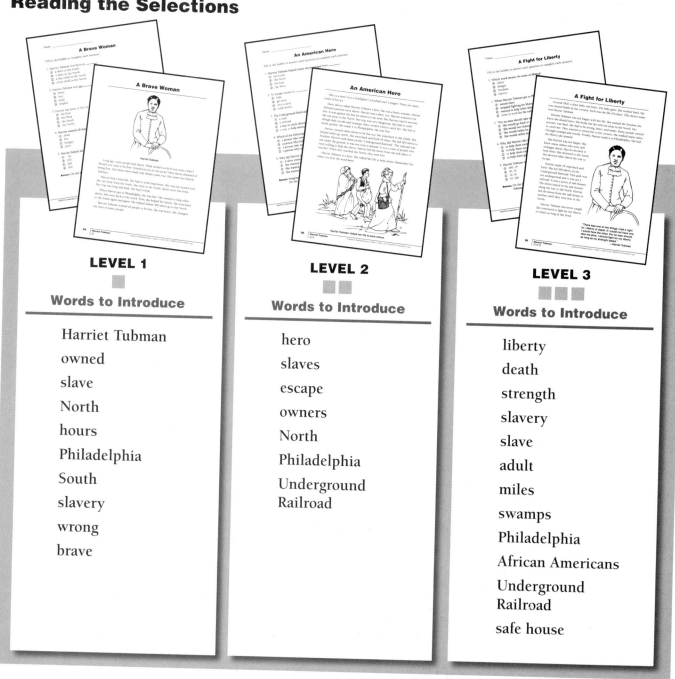

LEVEL 1

Words to Introduce

Harriet Tubman
owned
slave
North
hours
Philadelphia
South
slavery
wrong
brave

LEVEL 2

Words to Introduce

hero
slaves
escape
owners
North
Philadelphia
Underground Railroad

LEVEL 3

Words to Introduce

liberty
death
strength
slavery
slave
adult
miles
swamps
Philadelphia
African Americans
Underground Railroad
safe house

Nonfiction Reading Practice, Grade 2 • EMC 3313 • ©2003 by Evan-Moor Corp.

Harriet Tubman's Escape to Freedom

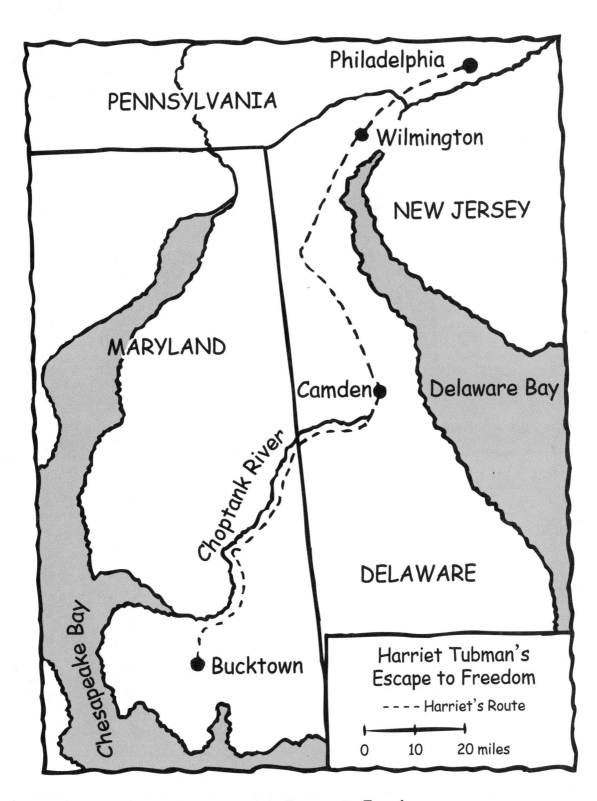

PENNSYLVANIA

Philadelphia

Wilmington

NEW JERSEY

MARYLAND

Camden

Delaware Bay

Choptank River

DELAWARE

Chesapeake Bay

Bucktown

Harriet Tubman's
Escape to Freedom

- - - - Harriet's Route

0   10   20 miles

Harriet Tubman's Escape to Freedom

A Brave Woman

Harriet Tubman

Long ago, some people had slaves. What would you do if you were a slave? Would you want to be free? Would you try to run away? Most slaves dreamed of being free. One brave slave made that dream come true. Her name was Harriet Tubman.

Harriet had a hard life. She had to work long hours. She was not treated well. She ran away from the South. She went to the North. Slaves were free there. Her trip was long and hard. She had to hide.

When Harriet got to Philadelphia, she was free! She wanted to help other slaves. She went back to the South. First, she helped her family. She went back to the South again and again. She helped almost 300 slaves go to the North.

Harriet Tubman wanted all people to be free. She was brave. She changed the lives of many people.

Nonfiction Reading Practice, Grade 2 • EMC 3313 • ©2003 by Evan-Moor Corp.

Name _____

A Brave Woman

Fill in the bubble to complete each sentence.

1. Harriet Tubman was born as _____.
   - (A) a slave in the South
   - (B) a slave in the North
   - (C) a free child in the South
   - (D) a free child in the North

2. Harriet Tubman was <u>not</u> _____.
   - (A) brave
   - (B) lazy
   - (C) kind
   - (D) helpful

3. Harriet ran away to live in _____.
   - (A) the East
   - (B) the West
   - (C) the South
   - (D) the North

4. Harriet wanted all slaves to be _____.
   - (A) alone
   - (B) free
   - (C) hungry
   - (D) poor

5. Harriet helped about _____ slaves.
   - (A) 30
   - (B) 100
   - (C) 200
   - (D) 300

Bonus: On the back of this page, tell what Harriet Tubman did that was brave.

An American Hero

Who is a hero? Is it a firefighter? a football star? a singer? There are many kinds of heroes.

Many slaves called Harriet Tubman a hero. She was a brave woman. Harriet Tubman's parents were slaves. Harriet was a slave, too. Harriet wanted to be free. It was against the law for slaves to run away. But Harriet tried it anyway. She ran away to the North. Her trip was very dangerous. She had to walk though dark woods and swamps. Slave owners tried to catch her. She had to think quickly. She made it to Philadelphia. She was free!

Harriet wanted other slaves to be free, too. She went back to the South. She helped others go north. She went back and forth 19 times. She led 300 slaves to freedom. Harriet took them on the "Underground Railroad." The railroad was not under the ground. It was not even a railroad. It was a team of people who were willing to help the slaves. Harriet led the slaves from one safe place to another. When they reached the North, they were free.

Harriet Tubman is a hero. She risked her life to help others. Remember her when you hear the word **hero**.

Harriet Tubman risked her life to save others.

Nonfiction Reading Practice, Grade 2 • EMC 3313 • ©2003 by Evan-Moor Corp.

Name _____

An American Hero

Fill in the bubble to answer each question or complete each sentence.

1. Harriet Tubman helped many slaves escape from _____.
   - Ⓐ the South
   - Ⓑ the North
   - Ⓒ the East
   - Ⓓ the West

2. To **escape** means to _____.
   - Ⓐ hide
   - Ⓑ get away
   - Ⓒ own a slave
   - Ⓓ walk slowly

3. The Underground Railroad was _____.
   - Ⓐ a road
   - Ⓑ a railroad
   - Ⓒ a way to catch slaves
   - Ⓓ a way to help slaves escape

4. Which of the following is the **hero**?
   - Ⓐ a person who owns slaves
   - Ⓑ a person who helps other people
   - Ⓒ a person who works for people
   - Ⓓ a person who teases people

5. Why did Harriet go back to the South?
   - Ⓐ A slave owner caught her.
   - Ⓑ She wanted to be free.
   - Ⓒ She wanted to help other slaves escape.
   - Ⓓ She wanted to see her friends.

Bonus: Imagine that you want to tell a friend about Harriet Tubman. On the back of this page, write what you would say.

A Fight for Liberty

Around 1820, a slave baby was born. The baby grew. She worked hard. She was treated badly by her owners. Such was the life of a slave. This slave's name was Harriet Tubman.

Harriet Tubman was not happy with her life. She wanted the freedom she knew she should have. She broke the law and ran away to the North. Her journey was hard. She had to be strong, brave, and smart. Many people wanted to catch her. They wanted to return her to her owners. She walked many miles through swamps and woods. Finally, Harriet made it to Philadelphia. She had the liberty she wanted.

But Harriet was not happy. She knew many others who were still unhappy slaves. Harriet decided to help them. She returned to the South. She showed other slaves the way to escape.

Harriet made 19 trips back and forth. She led 300 slaves on the Underground Railroad. This path was not underground and it was not a railroad. It was a series of safe houses. The slaves stayed in the safe houses along the way to the North. Harriet led the slaves from one safe house to another until they were free in the North.

Harriet Tubman was never caught. She continued to fight for the liberty of others as long as she lived.

"There was one of two things I had a right to—liberty or death. If I could not have one, I would have the other. For no man should take me alive. I should fight for my liberty as long as my strength lasted."
—Harriet Tubman

Nonfiction Reading Practice, Grade 2 • EMC 3313 • ©2003 by Evan-Moor Corp.

Name _____

A Fight for Liberty

Fill in the bubble to answer each question or complete each sentence.

1. Which word means the same as **liberty**?
   - Ⓐ safety
   - Ⓑ danger
   - Ⓒ freedom
   - Ⓓ slavery

2. When Harriet Tubman got to Philadelphia, she _____.
   - Ⓐ stayed there
   - Ⓑ stopped fighting for liberty
   - Ⓒ wanted to help other slaves
   - Ⓓ went to work for the railroad

3. "For no man should take me alive." What did Harriet mean?
   - Ⓐ She would go back to the South if she was caught.
   - Ⓑ She would not chance going back to the South.
   - Ⓒ She would rather be a slave than dead.
   - Ⓓ She would rather be dead than a slave.

4. Why did Harriet take slaves on the Underground Railroad?
   - Ⓐ to help them escape to the North
   - Ⓑ to help them escape to the South
   - Ⓒ to help them ride the train
   - Ⓓ to help them go under the ground to hide

5. Harriet Tubman made _____ trips to the South to help _____ slaves.
   - Ⓐ 300, 19
   - Ⓑ 30, 19
   - Ⓒ 19, 30
   - Ⓓ 19, 300

Bonus: On the back of this page, write a paragraph that tells about Harriet Tubman's bravery.

The California Gold Rush

Introducing the Topic

1. Reproduce page 31 for individual students, or make a transparency to use with a group or your whole class.

2. Show the early methods of mining for gold to the students. Point out the special equipment used. Talk about how difficult the whole mining process must have been for the miners.

Reading the Selections

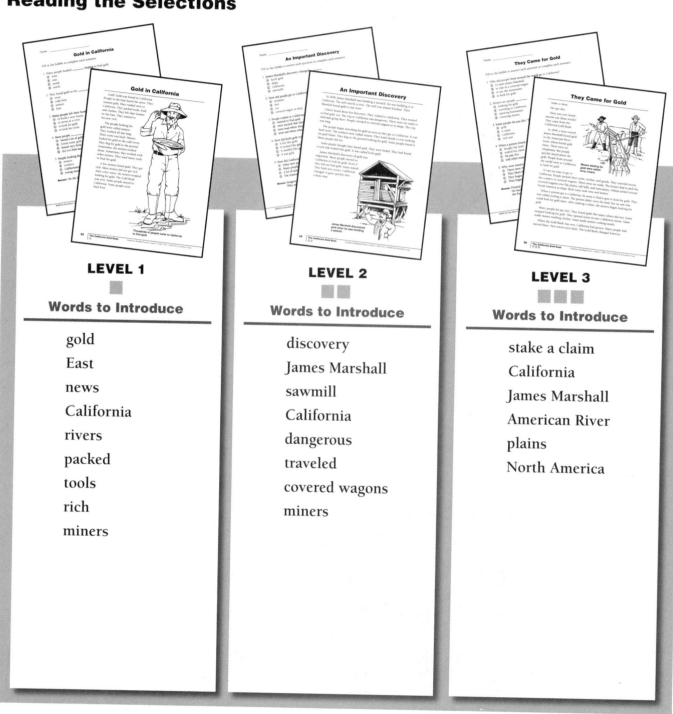

LEVEL 1
Words to Introduce

gold
East
news
California
rivers
packed
tools
rich
miners

LEVEL 2
Words to Introduce

discovery
James Marshall
sawmill
California
dangerous
traveled
covered wagons
miners

LEVEL 3
Words to Introduce

stake a claim
California
James Marshall
American River
plains
North America

Nonfiction Reading Practice, Grade 2 • EMC 3313 • ©2003 by Evan-Moor Corp.

The California Gold Rush

The miners are working with two basic tools—a **pan** and a **rocker**—to separate gold nuggets from gravel and sand.

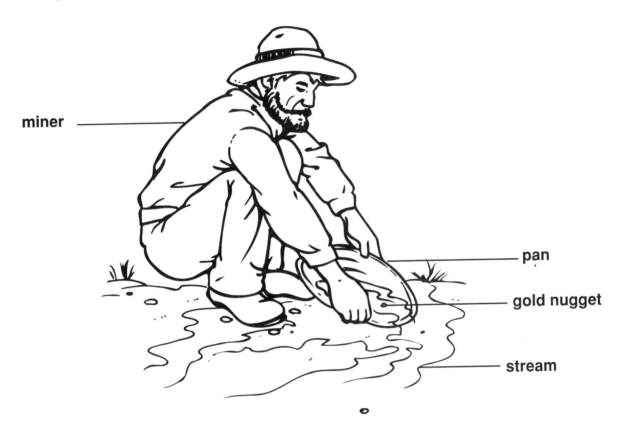

miner

pan

gold nugget

stream

miner

miner

miner

stream

rocker

Gold in California

Gold! Gold was found in California. People in the East heard the news. They wanted gold. They rushed west to California. They packed tools, food, and clothes. They left their homes in the East. They wanted to become rich.

The people looking for gold were called miners. They worked all day long. Their work was hard. Miners looked for gold in the cold rivers. They dug for gold in the ground. Sometimes, the miners worked alone. Sometimes, they worked with other miners. They used many tools to find the gold.

A few miners found gold. They got rich. Most miners did not get rich. After a few years, the miners stopped looking for gold. The Gold Rush was over. Some people stayed in California. Some people went back East.

Thousands of people came to California to find gold.

The California Gold Rush   Nonfiction Reading Practice, Grade 2 • EMC 3313 • ©2003 by Evan-Moor Corp.

Name _____

Gold in California

Fill in the bubble to complete each sentence.

1. Many people headed _____ hoping to find gold.
   - Ⓐ west
   - Ⓑ east
   - Ⓒ south
   - Ⓓ north

2. They found gold in the _____.
   - Ⓐ trees
   - Ⓑ cold river
   - Ⓒ miners
   - Ⓓ East

3. Many people left their homes because they wanted _____.
   - Ⓐ to build a new house
   - Ⓑ to swim in a river
   - Ⓒ to look for gold
   - Ⓓ to look for rocks

4. Most people _____.
   - Ⓐ found a lot of gold
   - Ⓑ found some gold
   - Ⓒ found very little gold
   - Ⓓ did not find any gold

5. People looking for gold were called _____.
   - Ⓐ miners
   - Ⓑ workers
   - Ⓒ Californians
   - Ⓓ young men

Bonus: On the back of this page, write about the Gold Rush.

An Important Discovery

In 1848, James Marshall was building a sawmill. He was building it in California. The mill was by a river. The mill was almost finished. Then Marshall found gold in the river!

Others heard about his discovery. They rushed to California. They wanted to find gold, too. The trip to California was dangerous. There were no roads or railroads going there. People traveled in covered wagons or in ships. The trip was long.

The people began searching for gold as soon as they got to California. It was hard work. The workers were called miners. They knelt beside a river looking for gold flakes. They dug in the ground looking for gold. Some people found it. Many people did not.

Some people thought they found gold. They were fooled. They had found a rock that looked like gold. It was called fool's gold.

James Marshall's discovery of gold was important. Many people moved to California to look for gold. Even if they did not find gold, many stayed. They built new towns. California changed. It grew quickly into a busy state.

James Marshall discovered gold when he was building a sawmill.

Nonfiction Reading Practice, Grade 2 • EMC 3313 • ©2003 by Evan-Moor Corp.

Name _____

An Important Discovery

Fill in the bubble to answer each question or complete each sentence.

1. James Marshall's discovery changed _____.
   - Ⓐ fool's gold
   - Ⓑ ships
   - Ⓒ California
   - Ⓓ sawmills

2. How did people get to California?
   - Ⓐ airplane
   - Ⓑ bus
   - Ⓒ car
   - Ⓓ covered wagon or ship

3. People rushed to California because they _____.
   - Ⓐ wanted to find gold
   - Ⓑ were excited that they found gold
   - Ⓒ were mad when they found fool's gold
   - Ⓓ were sad when others found gold

4. How did fool's gold trick the miners?
   - Ⓐ It felt like gold.
   - Ⓑ It looked like gold.
   - Ⓒ It smelled like gold.
   - Ⓓ It was gold.

5. How did California change during the Gold Rush?
   - Ⓐ Many new people moved there.
   - Ⓑ Many people left California.
   - Ⓒ A lot of sawmills were built.
   - Ⓓ The American River got colder.

Bonus: Imagine that you lived in 1849. Would you go to California to find gold? Why or why not?

They Came for Gold

Stake a claim.

Hit pay dirt.

Have you ever heard anyone use these words? They came from the California Gold Rush.

In 1849, a man named James Marshall found gold in the American River. Soon, others found gold there. There were no telephones. But people quickly heard about the gold. People from around the world went to California to look for gold.

Miners looking for gold were called forty-niners.

It was not easy to get to California. People packed their tools, clothes, and goods. They traveled across the country in covered wagons. There were no roads. The horses had to pull the covered wagons over flat plains, tall hills, and mountains. Others sailed around North America in ships. Both ways took time and money.

When a person got to California, he went to find a spot to look for gold. This was called staking a claim. The person didn't own the land, but no one else could look for gold there. After staking a claim, the miners began looking for gold.

Many people hit pay dirt. They found gold! But many others did not. Some stopped looking for gold. They opened stores in new California towns. Some made money washing clothes. Some made money cooking meals.

When the Gold Rush was over, California had grown. Many people had moved there. New towns were built. The Gold Rush changed America.

Nonfiction Reading Practice, Grade 2 • EMC 3313 • ©2003 by Evan-Moor Corp.

Name _____

They Came for Gold

Fill in the bubble to answer each question or complete each sentence.

1. Why did people from around the world go to California?
   - Ⓐ to meet James Marshall
   - Ⓑ to ride in a covered wagon
   - Ⓒ to see the mountains
   - Ⓓ to look for gold

2. Miners are people _____.
   - Ⓐ looking for gold
   - Ⓑ traveling to California
   - Ⓒ opening businesses
   - Ⓓ counting money

3. Some people hit pay dirt. What is **pay dirt**?
   - Ⓐ gold
   - Ⓑ a claim
   - Ⓒ California
   - Ⓓ rich soil

4. When a person found a place to look for gold, he _____.
   - Ⓐ bought the land
   - Ⓑ staked his claim
   - Ⓒ hit pay dirt
   - Ⓓ told other miners about it

5. Why were miners called **forty-niners**?
   - Ⓐ There were 49 miners.
   - Ⓑ They liked the name.
   - Ⓒ They began to search for gold in 1849.
   - Ⓓ They began to search for gold in 1949.

Bonus: Pretend that you lived in 1849. You went to California to find gold. On the back of this page, write a paragraph that tells about your trip from the East and your life in California. Did you find gold?

The Great Lakes

Introducing the Topic

1. Reproduce page 39 for individual students, or make a transparency to use with a group or your whole class.

2. Explore the map with students. Read the name of each lake and the surrounding states and provinces. Point out that the lakes are connected.

Reading the Selections

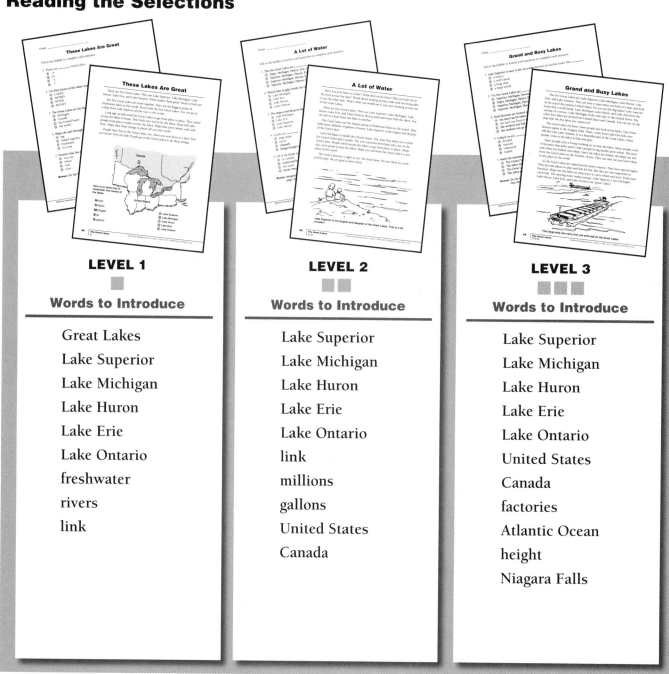

LEVEL 1

Words to Introduce

Great Lakes

Lake Superior

Lake Michigan

Lake Huron

Lake Erie

Lake Ontario

freshwater

rivers

link

LEVEL 2

Words to Introduce

Lake Superior

Lake Michigan

Lake Huron

Lake Erie

Lake Ontario

link

millions

gallons

United States

Canada

LEVEL 3

Words to Introduce

Lake Superior

Lake Michigan

Lake Huron

Lake Erie

Lake Ontario

United States

Canada

factories

Atlantic Ocean

height

Niagara Falls

Nonfiction Reading Practice, Grade 2 • EMC 3313 • ©2003 by Evan-Moor Corp.

Map of the Great Lakes

Canada

Ontario

Québec

St. Lawrence River

Minnesota

Wisconsin

(A)

(C)

Michigan

(E)

New York

(B)

(D)

Pennsylvania

Illinois

Indiana

Ohio

United States

(A) Lake Superior
(B) Lake Michigan
(C) Lake Huron
(D) Lake Erie
(E) Lake Ontario

These Lakes Are Great

There are five Great Lakes. They are Lake Superior, Lake Michigan, Lake Huron, Lake Erie, and Lake Ontario. What makes them great? Read to find out!

The five Great Lakes are close together. They are the biggest group of freshwater lakes in the world. Rivers link the five Great Lakes. You can go in a ship from Lake Superior all the way to the ocean.

Long ago, people used the Great Lakes to get from place to place. They sailed across the lakes in boats. They built new towns by the lakes. Ships still take people from place to place across the lakes. Ships also carry wheat, coal, and flour. Ships take these things to places all over the world.

People have fun in the Great Lakes, too. Have you ever been to a lake? Did you swim? Did you fish? People go to the Great Lakes to do these things.

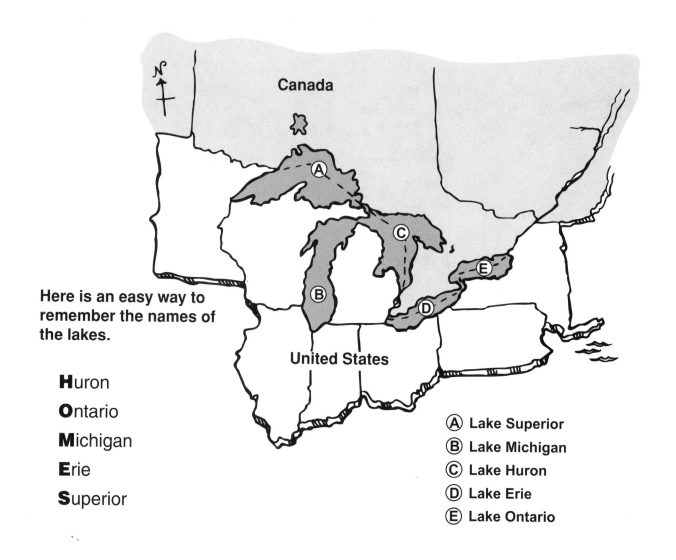

Here is an easy way to remember the names of the lakes.

Huron

Ontario

Michigan

Erie

Superior

Ⓐ Lake Superior
Ⓑ Lake Michigan
Ⓒ Lake Huron
Ⓓ Lake Erie
Ⓔ Lake Ontario

Name _____

These Lakes Are Great

Fill in the bubble to complete each sentence.

1. There are _____ Great Lakes.
   - Ⓐ 4
   - Ⓑ 15
   - Ⓒ 5
   - Ⓓ 7

2. The first letters of the lakes' names spell _____.
   - Ⓐ LAKES
   - Ⓑ HOMES
   - Ⓒ RIVER
   - Ⓓ MONEY

3. The Great Lakes are the biggest group of freshwater lakes in _____.
   - Ⓐ Michigan
   - Ⓑ Canada
   - Ⓒ the United States
   - Ⓓ the world

4. Ships can sail through the Great Lakes because the lakes are all _____.
   - Ⓐ big
   - Ⓑ linked together
   - Ⓒ freshwater
   - Ⓓ in a row

5. Farmers that live near the Great Lakes grow _____.
   - Ⓐ iron ore
   - Ⓑ wheat
   - Ⓒ coal
   - Ⓓ corn

Bonus: On the back of this page, write the names of the Great Lakes.

A Lot of Water

Have you ever been to a lake? What did you do there? Did you look out at the trees across the lake? Think about looking across a lake and not being able to see the other side. That's what you would see if you were looking across one of the Great Lakes.

There are five Great Lakes. They are Lake Superior, Lake Michigan, Lake Huron, Lake Erie, and Lake Ontario. Rivers and waterways link the lakes. You can sail in a boat from one lake to another.

The Great Lakes are the largest group of freshwater lakes in the world. They hold many millions of gallons of water. Lake Superior is the largest and deepest of the Great Lakes.

Lake Michigan is inside the United States. The other four lakes are in both the United States and Canada. The two countries both help take care of the Great Lakes. People travel across the lakes to get from place to place. Ships also carry goods across the lakes. Ships can sail from the Great Lakes to any place in the world.

The Great Lakes are a sight to see. We need them. We use them for work and for play. We are glad to have them.

Lake Superior is the largest and deepest of the Great Lakes. That is a lot of water!

Nonfiction Reading Practice, Grade 2 • EMC 3313 • ©2003 by Evan-Moor Corp.

Name _____

A Lot of Water

Fill in the bubble to answer each question or complete each sentence.

1. The five Great Lakes are _____.
   - Ⓐ Super, Michigan, Henry, Erie, Ontario
   - Ⓑ Superior, Michigan, Huron, Erie
   - Ⓒ Superior, Michigan, Huron, Ear, Canada
   - Ⓓ Superior, Michigan, Huron, Erie, Ontario

2. Which lake is <u>only</u> inside the United States?
   - Ⓐ Lake Michigan
   - Ⓑ Lake Erie
   - Ⓒ Lake Huron
   - Ⓓ Lake Ontario

3. The largest and deepest lake is _____.
   - Ⓐ Lake Michigan
   - Ⓑ Lake Erie
   - Ⓒ Lake Superior
   - Ⓓ Lake Huron

4. **Goods** are _____.
   - Ⓐ large ships
   - Ⓑ rivers
   - Ⓒ channels
   - Ⓓ things bought and sold

5. All of the Great Lakes are _____.
   - Ⓐ in Canada
   - Ⓑ connected by water
   - Ⓒ salt water
   - Ⓓ warm water

Bonus: Imagine you are planning to visit the Great Lakes. On the back of this page, write what you would probably see once you got there.

Grand and Busy Lakes

The five Great Lakes are Lake Superior, Lake Michigan, Lake Huron, Lake Erie, and Lake Ontario. They are easy to spot when you look at a map. Just look at the top of the eastern United States. Do you see five big lakes? Lake Superior looks like a wolf's head. Lake Michigan, Lake Huron, and Lake Erie form the outline of a mitten. Lake Michigan is the only lake in the United States. The other four lakes are in both the United States and Canada. You can see on the map that the five lakes are connected.

The Great Lakes are busy. Some people just look at the lakes. One of the famous sights is the Niagara Falls. There, water from Lake Erie falls over 300 feet into Lake Ontario. It is a beautiful part of the Great Lakes. Other people come to the lakes to fish and play.

Many people earn a living working on or near the lakes. Many people work in factories that make steel. Other people living nearby grow wheat. The steel and wheat are loaded onto ships. Since the lakes are linked, the ships can sail from the Great Lakes to the Atlantic Ocean. They can take the steel and wheat to any place in the world.

So the Great Lakes are important for many reasons. They have special sights. They provide places to play and fish for fun. But they are also important to business. Ships use the lakes as waterways to carry wheat and steel. Fishermen catch fish. The moving water makes energy. Lake Superior, Lake Michigan, Lake Huron, Lake Erie, and Lake Ontario are "great" lakes!

This large ship can carry iron ore and coal on the Great Lakes.

Nonfiction Reading Practice, Grade 2 • EMC 3313 • ©2003 by Evan-Moor Corp.

Name _____

Grand and Busy Lakes

Fill in the bubble to answer each question or complete each sentence.

1. Lake Superior is easy to see on a map because its outline looks like _____.
   - Ⓐ a mitten
   - Ⓑ a wolf's head
   - Ⓒ a large ship
   - Ⓓ a large island

2. The five Great Lakes are _____.
   - Ⓐ Superior, Michigan, Huron, Ear, Canada
   - Ⓑ Super, Michigan, Henry, Erie, Ontario
   - Ⓒ Superior, Michigan, Huron, Erie
   - Ⓓ Superior, Michigan, Huron, Erie, Ontario

3. Steel factories are located near the Great Lakes so _____.
   - Ⓐ the steel can be taken to other places
   - Ⓑ the steel can float in the lakes
   - Ⓒ the workers can fish in the lakes
   - Ⓓ the workers can go home across the lakes

4. **Linked** means _____.
   - Ⓐ divided
   - Ⓑ enjoyed
   - Ⓒ connected
   - Ⓓ loaded

5. Mark the statement that is <u>not</u> true.
   - Ⓐ The United States and Canada made the Great Lakes.
   - Ⓑ The lakes are good for fishing.
   - Ⓒ The Great Lakes are connected by water.
   - Ⓓ The lakes are deep.

Bonus: On the back of this page, write a paragraph that tells why it is important that the Great Lakes are connected.

Magnets

Introducing the Topic

1. Reproduce page 47 for individual students, or make a transparency to use with a group or your whole class.

2. Point out the various shapes and sizes of the magnets. Have students predict items that a magnet can attract. Compare their predictions to the chart. Encourage students to add their own items to the chart.

Reading the Selections

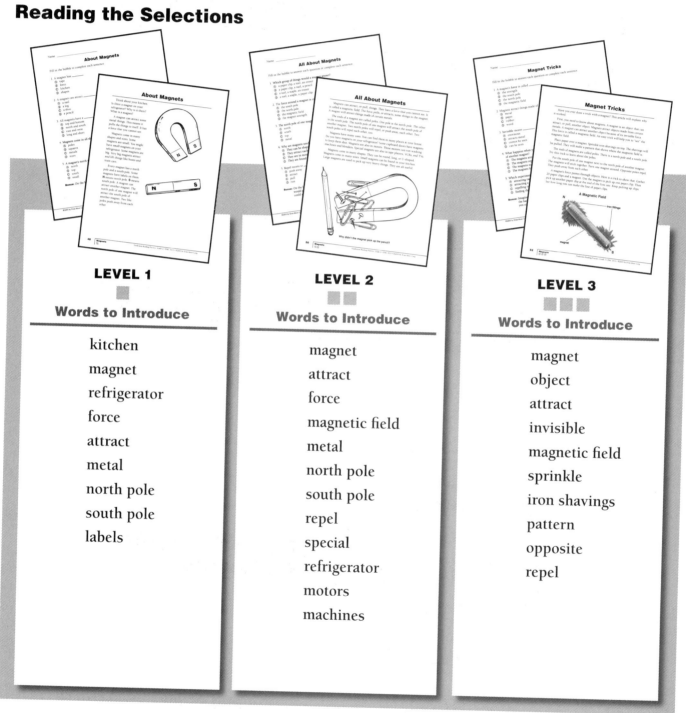

LEVEL 1

Words to Introduce

kitchen

magnet

refrigerator

force

attract

metal

north pole

south pole

labels

LEVEL 2

Words to Introduce

magnet

attract

force

magnetic field

metal

north pole

south pole

repel

special

refrigerator

motors

machines

LEVEL 3

Words to Introduce

magnet

object

attract

invisible

magnetic field

sprinkle

iron shavings

pattern

opposite

repel

Nonfiction Reading Practice, Grade 2 • EMC 3313 • ©2003 by Evan-Moor Corp.

Common Magnets

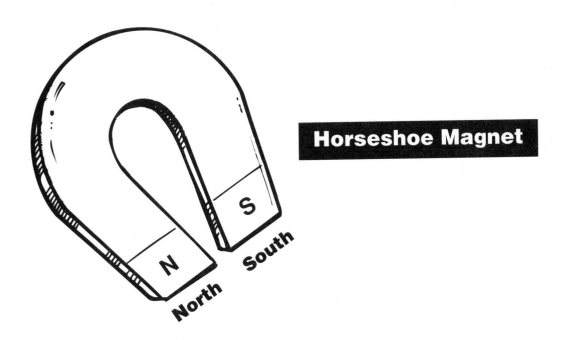

Horseshoe Magnet

North   South

Bar Magnet

North   South

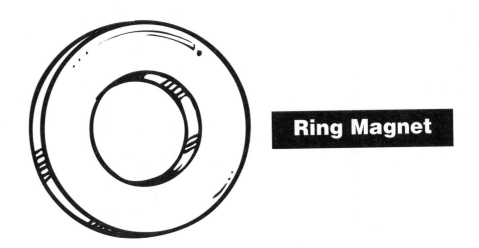

Ring Magnet

Magnets come in many shapes and sizes.

About Magnets

Think about your kitchen. Is there a magnet on your refrigerator? Why is it there? What is a magnet?

A magnet can attract some metal things. This means it pulls the things to itself. It has a force that you cannot see.

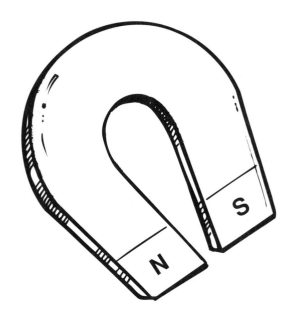

Magnets come in many shapes and sizes. Some magnets are small. You might have small magnets on your refrigerator. Some magnets are big. Very big magnets attract and lift things like buses and train cars.

Every magnet has a north pole and a south pole. Some magnets have labels on them. **N** means north pole. **S** means south pole. A magnet can attract another magnet. The north pole of one magnet will attract the south pole of another magnet. Two like, or the same, poles push away from each other.

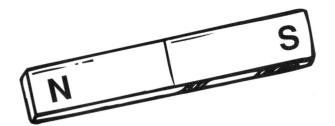

Nonfiction Reading Practice, Grade 2 • EMC 3313 • ©2003 by Evan-Moor Corp.

Name _____

About Magnets

Fill in the bubble to complete each sentence.

1. A magnet has _____.
   - Ⓐ tape
   - Ⓑ force
   - Ⓒ kitchen
   - Ⓓ shapes

2. A magnet can attract _____.
   - Ⓐ a nail
   - Ⓑ a log
   - Ⓒ a shoe
   - Ⓓ a pencil

3. All magnets have a _____ pole.
   - Ⓐ top and bottom
   - Ⓑ north and south
   - Ⓒ east and west
   - Ⓓ long and short

4. Magnets come in all shapes and _____.
   - Ⓐ poles
   - Ⓑ squares
   - Ⓒ metals
   - Ⓓ sizes

5. A magnet's north pole will attract the _____ pole of another magnet.
   - Ⓐ north
   - Ⓑ top
   - Ⓒ south
   - Ⓓ small

Bonus: On the back of this page, write some things that you learned about magnets.

All About Magnets

Magnets can attract, or pull, things. They have a force that you cannot see. It is called a magnetic field. The force pulls, or attracts, some things to the magnet. A magnet will attract things made of certain metals.

The ends of a magnet are called poles. One pole is the north pole. The other is the south pole. The north pole of one magnet will attract the south pole of another magnet. Two north poles will repel, or push away, each other. Two south poles will repel each other, too.

Magnets have many uses. You can find them in many places at your house. Do you have magnets on your refrigerator? Some cupboard doors have magnets to keep them shut. Magnets are also in motors. These motors can run washing machines and blenders. Special magnets are also in tape players, VCRs, and TVs.

Magnets come in many shapes. They can be round, long, or U-shaped. Magnets come in many sizes. Small magnets can be found in your kitchen. Large magnets are used to pick up very heavy things. They are all useful.

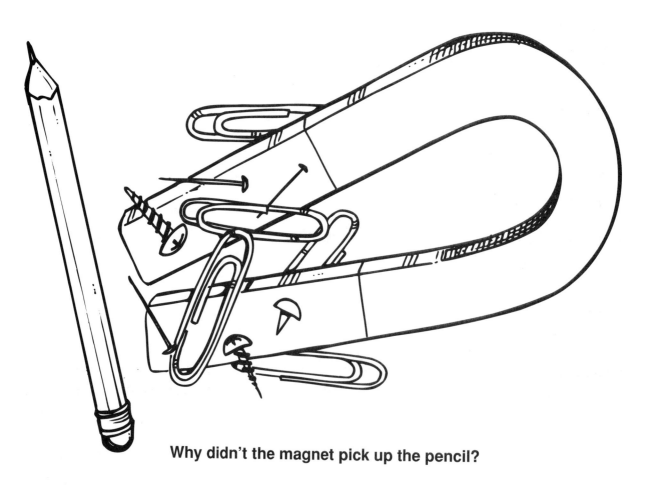

Why didn't the magnet pick up the pencil?

Nonfiction Reading Practice, Grade 2 • EMC 3313 • ©2003 by Evan-Moor Corp.

Name _____

All About Magnets

Fill in the bubble to answer each question or complete each sentence.

1. Which group of things would a magnet attract?
   - Ⓐ a paper clip, a nail, an eraser
   - Ⓑ a paper clip, a nail, a pencil
   - Ⓒ a nail, a staple, an eraser
   - Ⓓ a nail, a staple, a paper clip

2. The force around a magnet is called _____.
   - Ⓐ the south pole
   - Ⓑ the north pole
   - Ⓒ the magnetic field
   - Ⓓ the magnet strength

3. The north pole of one magnet will attract the _____ pole of another magnet.
   - Ⓐ north
   - Ⓑ south
   - Ⓒ top
   - Ⓓ metal

4. Why are magnets used on some cupboard doors?
   - Ⓐ They can be shaped like horseshoes.
   - Ⓑ They attract each other to hold the door shut.
   - Ⓒ They are in motors.
   - Ⓓ They are found in kitchens.

5. **Repel** means to _____.
   - Ⓐ push away
   - Ⓑ attract
   - Ⓒ pull
   - Ⓓ run

Bonus: On the back of this page, write a list of things in the room a magnet would pick up. Then make a list of things in the room that a magnet could not pick up.

Magnet Tricks

Have you ever done a trick with a magnet? This article will explain why it worked.

First, you need to know about magnets. A magnet is an object that can attract, or pull, another object. Magnets attract objects made from certain metals. A magnet can attract another object because of its invisible force. This force is called a magnetic field. An easy trick will help you to "see" the magnetic field.

Place paper over a magnet. Sprinkle iron shavings on top. The shavings will be pulled. They will make a pattern that shows where the magnetic field is.

The ends of magnets are called poles. There is a north pole and a south pole. Try this trick to learn about the poles.

Put the south pole of one magnet next to the north pole of another magnet. The magnets will stick together. Turn one magnet around. Opposite poles repel. They push away from each other.

A magnet's force passes through objects. Here is a trick to show that. Gather 20 paper clips and a magnet. Use the magnet to pick up one paper clip. Then pick up another paper clip at the end of the first one. Keep picking up clips. See how long you can make the line of paper clips.

A Magnetic Field

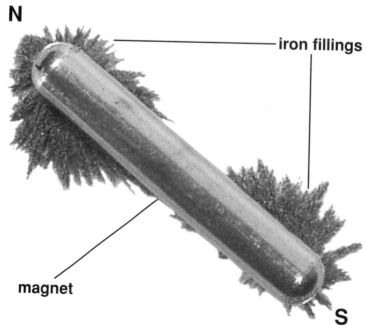

N

iron fillings

magnet

S

Nonfiction Reading Practice, Grade 2 • EMC 3313 • ©2003 by Evan-Moor Corp.

Name _____

Magnet Tricks

Fill in the bubble to answer each question or complete each sentence.

1. A magnet's **force** is called _____.
   - Ⓐ the strength
   - Ⓑ the south pole
   - Ⓒ the north pole
   - Ⓓ the magnetic field

2. Magnets attract things made of _____.
   - Ⓐ metal
   - Ⓑ paper
   - Ⓒ rubber
   - Ⓓ wood

3. **Invisible** means _____.
   - Ⓐ enormous
   - Ⓑ attracts metal
   - Ⓒ cannot be seen
   - Ⓓ can be seen

4. What happens when you put the north pole of one magnet next to the south pole of another magnet?
   - Ⓐ The magnets attract.
   - Ⓑ The magnets repel.
   - Ⓒ The magnets stay the same.
   - Ⓓ The magnets look different.

5. Which experiment proves that a magnet's force can go through an object?
   - Ⓐ attracting two magnets
   - Ⓑ attracting a line of paper clips
   - Ⓒ repelling two magnets
   - Ⓓ finding the pattern of the field lines

Bonus: Imagine that you will do a show of magnet tricks for your friends. On the back of this page, write a paragraph that explains a magnet trick you could do.

©2003 by Evan-Moor Corp. • Nonfiction Reading Practice, Grade 2 • EMC 3313

Magnets | **53**

Desert Habitat

Introducing the Topic

1. Reproduce the map on page 55 for individual students, or make a transparency to use with a group or your whole class.

2. Explain the map to students. Point out the different desert areas of the world. Help students understand that deserts are dry. But temperatures can range from scorching hot to freezing cold, depending on the elevation of the land. Read the Fun Facts together to highlight interesting details about deserts.

Reading the Selections

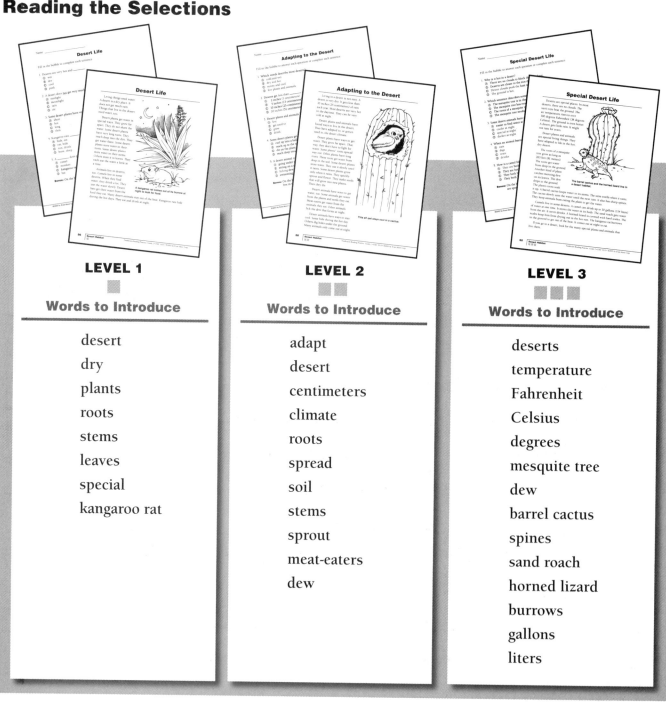

LEVEL 1	LEVEL 2	LEVEL 3
Words to Introduce	**Words to Introduce**	**Words to Introduce**
desert	adapt	deserts
dry	desert	temperature
plants	centimeters	Fahrenheit
roots	climate	Celsius
stems	roots	degrees
leaves	spread	mesquite tree
special	soil	dew
kangaroo rat	stems	barrel cactus
	sprout	spines
	meat-eaters	sand roach
	dew	horned lizard
		burrows
		gallons
		liters

Nonfiction Reading Practice, Grade 2 • EMC 3313 • ©2003 by Evan-Moor Corp.

Desert Fun Facts

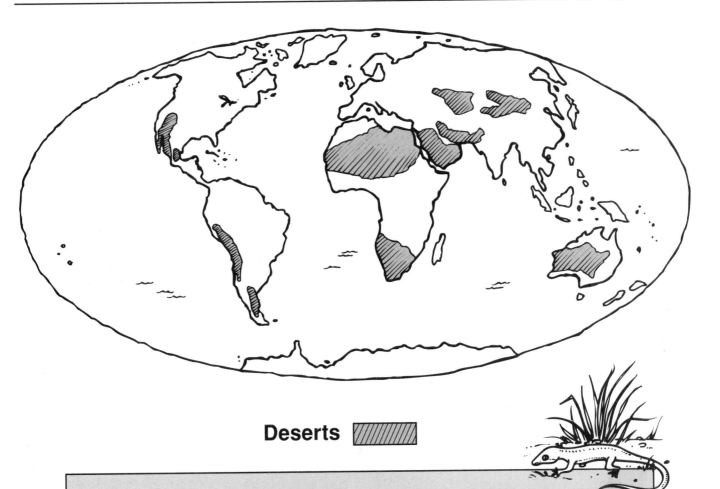

Deserts

- Deserts cover about one-fifth of the Earth's land.
- Deserts get less than 10 inches
  (25 centimeters) of rain each year.
- There are four types of deserts: hot and dry,
  semiarid, coastal, and cold.
- The largest desert in the world is the Sahara
  Desert in Africa. It is about the size of the
  United States.

Desert Life

Living things need water. A desert is a dry place. It does not get much rain. Things that live in the desert need water, too.

Desert plants get water in special ways. They grow far apart. They do not share the water. Some desert plants have very long roots. They reach deep into the dirt. They get water there. Some desert plants store water in their roots. Some desert plants store water in their stems. Others store it in leaves. They each use the water a little at a time.

Animals live in deserts, too. Camels live in some deserts. When they find water, they drink a lot. They use the water slowly. Desert bats get their water from the food they eat. Many desert animals stay out of the heat. Kangaroo rats hide during the hot days. They eat and drink at night.

A kangaroo rat comes out of its burrow at night to look for food.

Nonfiction Reading Practice, Grade 2 • EMC 3313 • ©2003 by Evan-Moor Corp.

Name _____

Desert Life

Fill in the bubble to complete each sentence.

1. Deserts are very hot and _____.
   - Ⓐ wet
   - Ⓑ dry
   - Ⓒ cool
   - Ⓓ pink

2. A desert does not get very much _____.
   - Ⓐ sunlight
   - Ⓑ moonlight
   - Ⓒ rain
   - Ⓓ air

3. Some desert plants have very _____ roots.
   - Ⓐ short
   - Ⓑ hot
   - Ⓒ long
   - Ⓓ thin

4. Kangaroo rats _____ during the day and _____ at night.
   - Ⓐ hide, eat
   - Ⓑ eat, hide
   - Ⓒ run, drink
   - Ⓓ hunt, sleep

5. A _____ does not live in the desert.
   - Ⓐ camel
   - Ⓑ monkey
   - Ⓒ kangaroo rat
   - Ⓓ bat

Bonus: On the back of this page, tell what you learned about desert plants.

Adapting to the Desert

Living in a desert is not easy. A desert is very dry. It gets less than 10 inches (25 centimeters) of rain each year. Most deserts are very hot in the daytime. They can be very cold at night.

Desert plants and animals have found ways to live in the desert. They have adapted to, or gotten used to, the desert climate.

Desert plants have ways to get water. They grow far apart. That way, they don't have to fight for water. Some plants' roots spread way out. Other plants have long roots. These roots get water from deep in the soil. Some desert plants store water. They use it slowly until it rains. Some desert plants grow only when it rains. They quickly sprout and flower. They make seeds that will grow into new plants. Then they die.

Desert animals have ways to get water, too. Some animals get water from the plants and seeds they eat. Meat-eaters get water from the animals they eat. Other animals lick the dew that forms at night.

Desert animals have ways to stay cool. Some hide during the hot day. Others dig holes under the ground. Many animals only come out at night.

This elf owl stays cool in a cactus.

Nonfiction Reading Practice, Grade 2 • EMC 3313 • ©2003 by Evan-Moor Corp.

Name _____

Adapting to the Desert

Fill in the bubble to answer each question or complete each sentence.

1. Which words describe most deserts?
   - Ⓐ cold and wet
   - Ⓑ dry and hot
   - Ⓒ sunny and cool
   - Ⓓ few plants and animals

2. Deserts get less than _____ of rain each year.
   - Ⓐ 2 inches (5 centimeters)
   - Ⓑ 5 inches (13 centimeters)
   - Ⓒ 10 inches (25 centimeters)
   - Ⓓ 20 inches (51 centimeters)

3. Desert plants and animals learn how to adapt. What does **adapt** mean?
   - Ⓐ live
   - Ⓑ get used to
   - Ⓒ grow
   - Ⓓ drink

4. Some desert plants get water by having their roots spread way out or _____.
   - Ⓐ curl up into a ball
   - Ⓑ reach up to the top of the soil
   - Ⓒ die on the plant
   - Ⓓ reach deep into the soil

5. A desert animal can <u>not</u> stay cool by _____.
   - Ⓐ going under the ground
   - Ⓑ sitting on a rock
   - Ⓒ licking dew
   - Ⓓ swimming in a pond

Bonus: On the back of this page, tell something you learned about animals that live in the desert.

Special Desert Life

Deserts are special places. In most deserts, there are no clouds. The sun's rays heat the ground. The air temperature rises to over 100 degrees Fahrenheit (38 degrees Celsius). The ground is even hotter. A desert gets little rain. It might not rain for years.

Desert plants and animals are special living things. They have adapted to life in the hot, dry desert.

The roots of a mesquite tree grow as long as 263 feet (81 meters). The roots get water from deep in the ground. Another kind of plant catches morning dew on its leaves. The dew drips to the ground. The plant's roots soak

The barrel cactus and the horned lizard live in a desert habitat.

it up. A barrel cactus keeps water in its stems. The stem swells when it rains. The cactus slowly uses the water until the next rain. It also has sharp spines. They keep animals from eating the plant to get the water.

Camels live in some deserts. A camel can drink up to 30 gallons (114 liters) of water at one time. It stores the water in its body. The sand roach gets water from the air. It never drinks. A horned lizard is covered with hard scales. The scales keep him from drying out in the hot sun. The kangaroo rat burrows in the ground to get out of the heat. It comes out at night to eat.

If you go to a desert, look for the many special plants and animals that live there.

Nonfiction Reading Practice, Grade 2 • EMC 3313 • ©2003 by Evan-Moor Corp.

Name _____

Special Desert Life

Fill in the bubble to answer each question or complete each sentence.

1. Why is it hot in a desert?
   - Ⓐ There are no clouds to block the sun's heat.
   - Ⓑ Deserts are closer to the sun than other places.
   - Ⓒ Desert clouds push the heat to the ground.
   - Ⓓ The ground is hot.

2. Which sentence describes something special about the mesquite tree?
   - Ⓐ The mesquite tree is in the desert.
   - Ⓑ The mesquite tree has roots.
   - Ⓒ The roots of a mesquite tree grow up to 263 feet (81 meters) long.
   - Ⓓ The mesquite tree needs water to grow.

3. Some desert animals hunt and eat at night because it is _____.
   - Ⓐ easier to find water at night
   - Ⓑ cooler at night
   - Ⓒ special at night
   - Ⓓ darker at night

4. When an animal **burrows**, it _____.
   - Ⓐ eats
   - Ⓑ digs
   - Ⓒ rests
   - Ⓓ drinks

5. How is a camel like a barrel cactus?
   - Ⓐ They are both animals.
   - Ⓑ They are both plants.
   - Ⓒ They both hold water.
   - Ⓓ They both have spines.

Bonus: On the back of this page, write about two desert plants. Tell how they are special.

Phases of the Moon

Introducing the Topic

1. Reproduce page 63 for individual students, or make a transparency to use with a group or your whole class.

2. Walk students through the diagram of the phases of the moon. Help them understand that the amount of reflected light from the sun determines the moon's appearance.

Reading the Selections

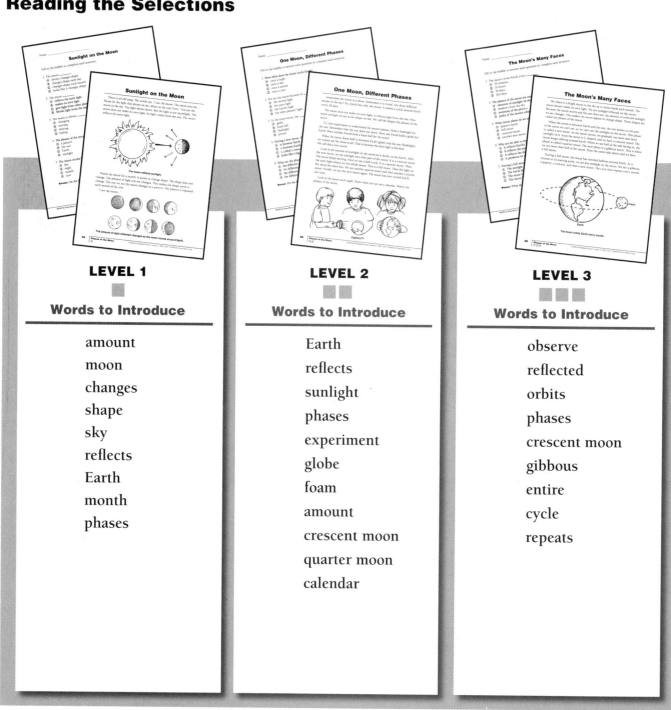

LEVEL 1
Words to Introduce

amount

moon

changes

shape

sky

reflects

Earth

month

phases

LEVEL 2
Words to Introduce

Earth

reflects

sunlight

phases

experiment

globe

foam

amount

crescent moon

quarter moon

calendar

LEVEL 3
Words to Introduce

observe

reflected

orbits

phases

crescent moon

gibbous

entire

cycle

repeats

Nonfiction Reading Practice, Grade 2 • EMC 3313 • ©2003 by Evan-Moor Corp.

Phases of the Moon

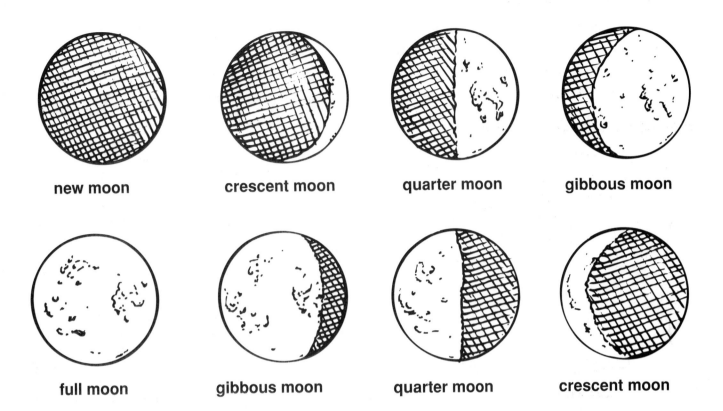

new moon   crescent moon   quarter moon   gibbous moon

full moon   gibbous moon   quarter moon   crescent moon

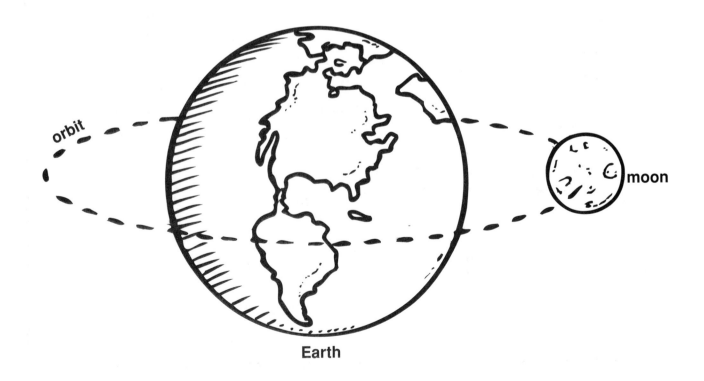

orbit

moon

Earth

Sunlight on the Moon

There is an old song. The words say, "I see the moon. The moon sees me.... Please let the light that shines on me, shine on the one I love." You see the moon in the sky. The light shines down. But the light is not moonlight. The moon does not make its own light. Its light comes from the sun. The moon reflects the sun's light.

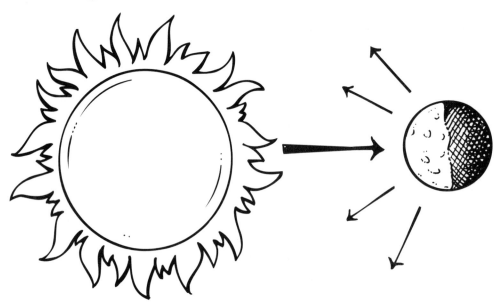

The moon reflects sunlight.

Watch the moon for a month. It seems to change shape. The shape does not change. The amount of light you see changes. This makes the shape seem to change. The way we see the moon changes in a pattern. The pattern is repeated each month of the year.

"I see the moon...."

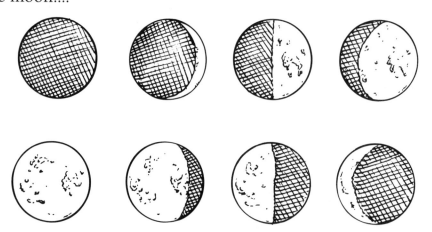

The amount of light reflected changes as the moon moves around Earth.

Nonfiction Reading Practice, Grade 2 • EMC 3313 • ©2003 by Evan-Moor Corp.

Name _____

Sunlight on the Moon

Fill in the bubble to complete each sentence.

1. The moon _____.
   - Ⓐ always changes shape
   - Ⓑ changes shape each day
   - Ⓒ changes shape each month
   - Ⓓ looks like it changes shape

2. The moon _____.
   - Ⓐ reflects the sun's light
   - Ⓑ makes its own light
   - Ⓒ gets light from other planets
   - Ⓓ blocks light from the sun

3. The moon is always _____.
   - Ⓐ changing
   - Ⓑ moving
   - Ⓒ shining
   - Ⓓ hiding

4. The phases of the moon follow _____.
   - Ⓐ a pattern
   - Ⓑ the sun
   - Ⓒ Earth
   - Ⓓ sunlight

5. The moon circles Earth one time every _____.
   - Ⓐ day
   - Ⓑ night
   - Ⓒ month
   - Ⓓ year

Bonus: On the back of this page, draw and label the phases of the moon.

One Moon, Different Phases

Sometimes the moon is a sliver. Sometimes it is round. Are there different moons in the sky? No, Earth has only one moon. It makes a circle around Earth every 30 days.

The moon does not make its own light. It reflects light from the sun. How much sunlight we see is the shape we see. We call the shapes the phases of the moon.

Try this experiment to understand the moon's phases. Hold a flashlight for the sun. Remember that the sun does not move. Have one friend hold a globe for the Earth. Have another friend hold a foam ball for the moon.

When the moon (foam ball) is between Earth (globe) and the sun (flashlight), we cannot see the moon at all. That is because the sun's light is blocked. We call this a new moon.

Look at the amount of sunlight on the moon as it slowly circles Earth. After the new moon, we see sunlight on a thin part of the moon. It is a crescent moon. The moon keeps moving. Next, we see a half circle. It is a quarter moon. Then the sun's light shines on the whole moon. This is a full moon. Then the light on the moon becomes less. We see another quarter moon and then another crescent moon. Finally, we see the new moon again. The moon has now circled Earth one time.

Look at the moon each night. Draw what you see on a calendar. Watch the phases of the moon.

Nonfiction Reading Practice, Grade 2 • EMC 3313 • ©2003 by Evan-Moor Corp.

Name _____

One Moon, Different Phases

Fill in the bubble to answer each question or complete each sentence.

1. How often does the moon circle Earth?
    - Ⓐ once a night
    - Ⓑ once a day
    - Ⓒ once a month
    - Ⓓ once a year

2. We see the moon because of _____.
    - Ⓐ the moon's light
    - Ⓑ the sun's light
    - Ⓒ the Earth's light
    - Ⓓ the other planets' light

3. In the experiment, the _____ stands for the moon.
    - Ⓐ globe
    - Ⓑ foam ball
    - Ⓒ flashlight
    - Ⓓ person

4. During a new moon, the moon _____.
    - Ⓐ is between Earth and the sun
    - Ⓑ is between Earth and the stars
    - Ⓒ is called a crescent moon
    - Ⓓ looks like a big circle

5. What are the phases of the moon?
    - Ⓐ the different number of moons
    - Ⓑ the different colors of the moon
    - Ⓒ the different circles of the moon
    - Ⓓ the different ways the moon looks

Bonus: On the back of this page, explain what the picture shows.

The Moon's Many Faces

We observe a bright moon in the sky as it circles Earth each month. The moon doesn't make its own light. We see sunlight reflected on the moon. Because the moon moves and the sun does not, the amount of reflected sunlight we see changes. This makes the moon appear to change shape. These shapes are called the phases of the moon.

When the moon is between Earth and the sun, the sun shines on the part of the moon we can't see, so we can't see the sunlight on the moon. This phase is called a new moon. As the moon moves, we gradually see more and more sunlight on it. Soon the moon is C-shaped, and we have a crescent moon. The moon keeps orbiting around Earth. When we see half of the side facing us, the phase is called a quarter moon. The next phase is a gibbous moon. This is when we see more than half of the moon. Then the entire side shows and we have a full moon.

During a full moon, the moon has traveled halfway around Earth. As it returns to its starting point, we see less sunlight on the moon. We see a gibbous, a quarter, a crescent, and then a new moon. The cycle then repeats every month.

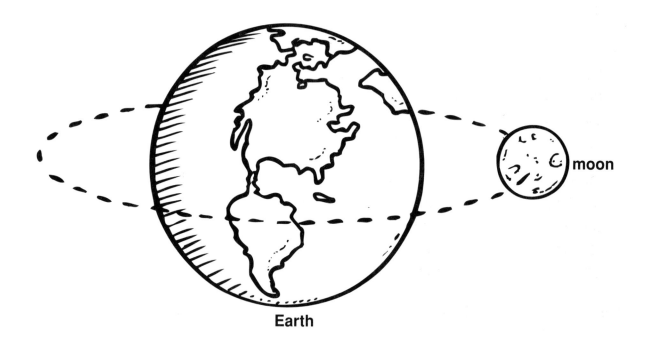

Earth

The moon orbits Earth every month.

Nonfiction Reading Practice, Grade 2 • EMC 3313 •

Name _____

The Moon's Many Faces

Fill in the bubble to answer each question or complete each sentence.

1. The moon circles Earth every _____.
   - (A) 30 minutes
   - (B) 24 hours
   - (C) 30 days
   - (D) 365 days

2. The phases of the moon are caused by different _____.
   - (A) amounts of sunlight on the moon
   - (B) shadows from the sky
   - (C) positions of the planets
   - (D) paths of the moon's orbit

3. What moon phase do we see after a new moon?
   - (A) quarter moon
   - (B) full moon
   - (C) crescent moon
   - (D) another new moon

4. Why are we able to see the moon in the night sky?
   - (A) It reflects Earth's light.
   - (B) It reflects the sun's light.
   - (C) It reflects the shadows.
   - (D) It produces its own light.

5. During a full moon, why does the moon look like a circle?
   - (A) The sunlight is directly on the moon.
   - (B) The Earth blocks the sunlight.
   - (C) The moon has circled Earth one time.
   - (D) The moon has made shadows over Earth.

Bonus: What does the movement of the moon have to do with our calendar?

Hubble Space Telescope

Introducing the Topic

1. Reproduce page 71 for individual students, or make a transparency to use with a group or your whole class.

2. Review the page with students. Point out Earth's position in the solar system compared to Pluto's. Show students where the Hubble space telescope is in the solar system, and point out the things in space that it can see.

Reading the Selections

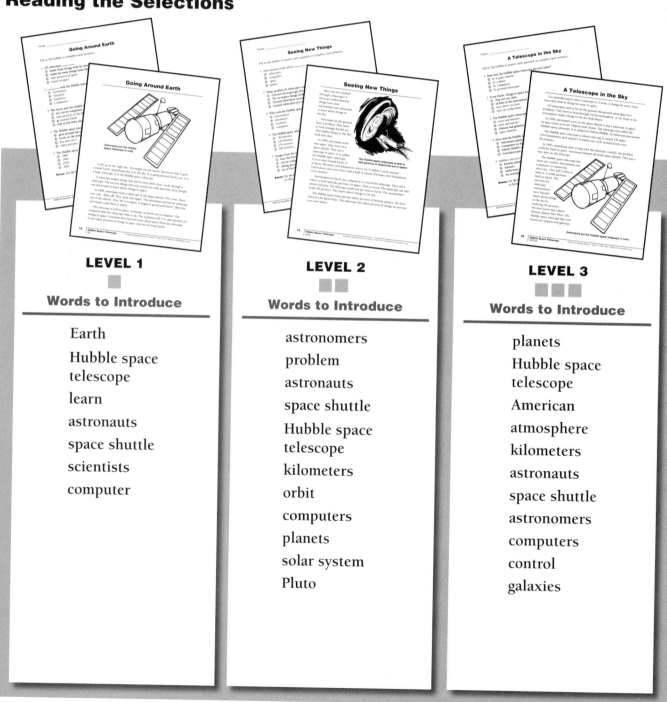

LEVEL 1

Words to Introduce

Earth

Hubble space telescope

learn

astronauts

space shuttle

scientists

computer

LEVEL 2

Words to Introduce

astronomers

problem

astronauts

space shuttle

Hubble space telescope

kilometers

orbit

computers

planets

solar system

Pluto

LEVEL 3

Words to Introduce

planets

Hubble space telescope

American

atmosphere

kilometers

astronauts

space shuttle

astronomers

computers

control

galaxies

Nonfiction Reading Practice, Grade 2 • EMC 3313 • ©2003 by Evan-Moor Corp.

Hubble Space Telescope

The Hubble space telescope takes clear pictures of things very far away. It can see all of the planets in our solar system. It can even see past our solar system.

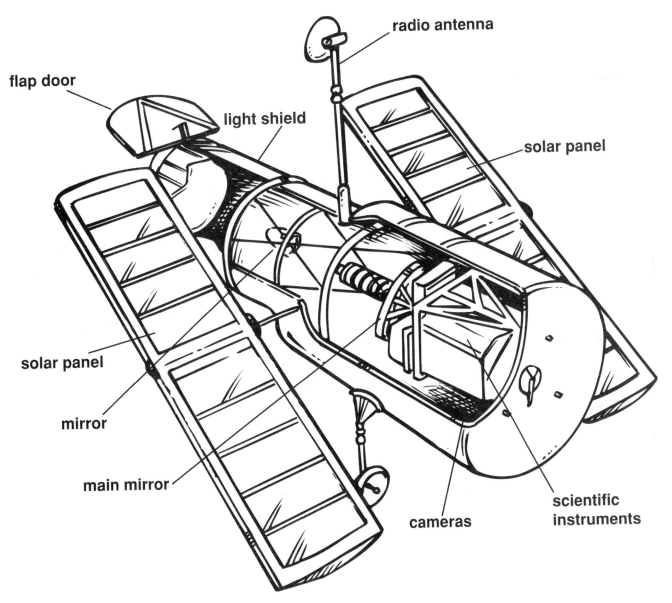

- The radio antenna sends signals to Earth.
- The flap door and light shield protect the instruments.
- The solar panels turn sunlight into power.
- The mirrors reflect the light to the instruments.
- The cameras take pictures far out in space.
- Scientific instruments are run by computers.

Going Around Earth

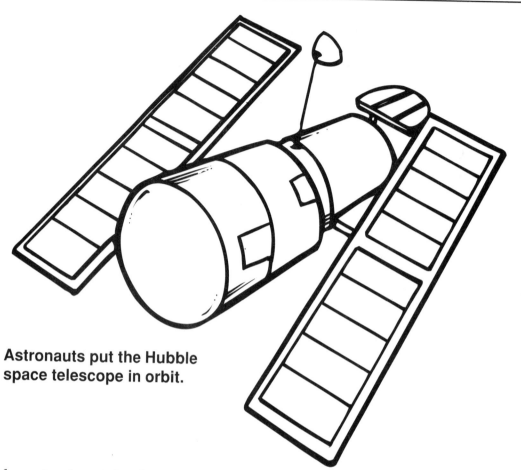

Astronauts put the Hubble space telescope in orbit.

Look up in the night sky. You might see the moon. You know that it goes around Earth. Something else is in the sky. It is going around Earth, too. It is a huge telescope. It is the Hubble space telescope.

A telescope makes things that are far away look close. Look through a telescope. You can see things that you cannot see with just your eyes. People use telescopes to learn about things in space.

In 1990, astronauts took a telescope in the space shuttle. Five, four, three, two, one…blast off! They went into space. The astronauts moved the telescope out of the shuttle. They left it in space. It began to go around Earth. Then the astronauts came back to Earth.

The telescope is still in space. Scientists on Earth use a computer. The computer tells the telescope what to do. The scientists tell it to take pictures of things in space. Scientists have learned more about space from the telescope. It has taken pictures of things in space that are far from Earth.

Name _____

Going Around Earth

Fill in the bubble to complete each sentence.

1. All telescopes _____.
   - Ⓐ make close things look far away
   - Ⓑ make far away things look close
   - Ⓒ take pictures of space
   - Ⓓ travel in space

2. _____ took the Hubble space telescope up into space.
   - Ⓐ Astronauts
   - Ⓑ Teachers
   - Ⓒ Explorers
   - Ⓓ Computers

3. The moon and the Hubble space telescope _____.
   - Ⓐ are run by computers
   - Ⓑ take pictures of the planets
   - Ⓒ go around Earth
   - Ⓓ stay in the same place

4. The Hubble space telescope _____.
   - Ⓐ goes around the sun
   - Ⓑ lands on the moon
   - Ⓒ has men on it
   - Ⓓ takes pictures

5. The Hubble space went into space in _____.
   - Ⓐ 1980
   - Ⓑ 1990
   - Ⓒ 2000
   - Ⓓ 2002

Bonus: On the back of this page, tell why the Hubble space telescope is important.

Seeing New Things

Have you ever looked through a telescope? A telescope makes faraway things look close. Astronomers use telescopes to learn about things in the sky.

Telescopes on the ground have a problem. They have to look through Earth's air. This makes things in the sky look less clear.

In 1990, astronauts went into space. They went on a space shuttle. They put a telescope in space. It is called the Hubble space telescope. It is in orbit around Earth. It is about 380 miles (610 kilometers) above us. It makes a circle around Earth about once every hour and a half. It travels 276 miles (444 kilometers) every minute!

The Hubble space telescope is able to take pictures of objects far out in space.

Astronomers on Earth use computers to control the telescope. They tell it where to look and take pictures. In space, there is no air. The telescope can take clearer pictures. The telescope sends the pictures to Earth. The astronomers study the pictures. They learn about things in the sky.

The Hubble space telescope has taken pictures of faraway planets. We have learned a lot about Pluto. The telescope has taken pictures of things no one has ever seen before.

Nonfiction Reading Practice, Grade 2 • EMC 3313 • ©2003 by Evan-Moor Corp.

Name _____

Seeing New Things

Fill in the bubble to answer each question or complete each sentence.

1. Astronomers study about _____.
   - Ⓐ telescopes
   - Ⓑ computers
   - Ⓒ space
   - Ⓓ plants

2. What problem do telescopes on the ground have?
   - Ⓐ Ground telescopes get dirty.
   - Ⓑ The air makes things look less clear.
   - Ⓒ Ground telescopes cannot see very far away.
   - Ⓓ Ground telescopes are too small.

3. Who took the Hubble space telescope up into space?
   - Ⓐ astronomers
   - Ⓑ astronauts
   - Ⓒ scientists
   - Ⓓ computers

4. The Hubble space telescope orbits Earth once every _____.
   - Ⓐ 90 minutes
   - Ⓑ 120 minutes
   - Ⓒ 276 minutes
   - Ⓓ 380 minutes

5. Images from the Hubble space telescope are clear because it is _____.
   - Ⓐ near the Earth
   - Ⓑ run by computers
   - Ⓒ taking pictures
   - Ⓓ out of Earth's air

Bonus: On the back of this page, tell how the Hubble space telescope knows what to take pictures of in space.

A Telescope in the Sky

You probably know what a telescope is. It looks at things far away. Some telescopes look at things far away in space.

All telescopes used to be on the ground. But ground telescopes have problems. They have to look through Earth's atmosphere, or air. Dust in the atmosphere makes things in the sky look blurry.

In 1990, astronauts went on the space shuttle to put a telescope in space. In space, there is no air. Objects look clearer. The telescope is called the Hubble space telescope. It is named for Edwin Hubble, an American astronomer.

The Hubble space telescope is always moving. It travels 276 miles (444 kilometers) each minute! It makes one circle around Earth every 96 minutes.

In 1993, something went wrong with the telescope. Luckily, the problem could be fixed in space. Astronauts blasted off in the space shuttle. They put a new part on the telescope.

The Hubble space telescope has been very useful. Astronomers use computers to control the telescope. They tell it what to look at. It sends pictures back to Earth. The pictures are amazing! Astronomers have learned much about things in the sky by studying the pictures. We now know more about faraway planets like Pluto. The Hubble space telescope has even found new planets and galaxies.

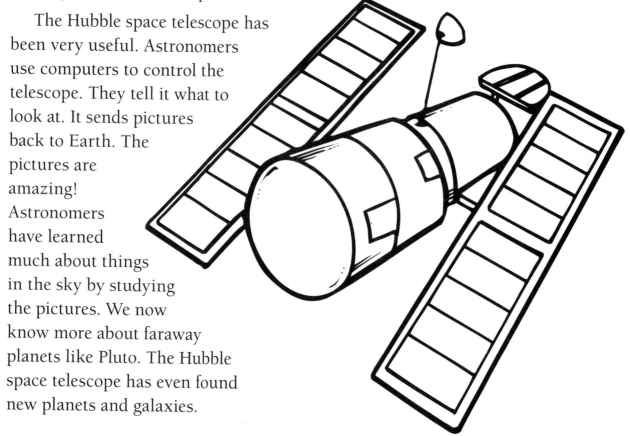

Astronauts put the Hubble space telescope in orbit.

Name _____

A Telescope in the Sky

Fill in the bubble to answer each question or complete each sentence.

1. How was the Hubble space telescope put into space?
   - Ⓐ by a space shuttle
   - Ⓑ by a plane
   - Ⓒ by computers
   - Ⓓ by ground telescopes

2. From Earth, things in space look blurry because _____.
   - Ⓐ they are too close
   - Ⓑ of dust in the atmosphere
   - Ⓒ they move too slow
   - Ⓓ they are underwater

3. The Hubble space telescope has sent back pictures of Pluto and new _____.
   - Ⓐ stars and meteors
   - Ⓑ suns and moons
   - Ⓒ planets and galaxies
   - Ⓓ space shuttles

4. How was the Hubble space telescope repaired?
   - Ⓐ Astronauts painted it.
   - Ⓑ Computers on Earth fixed it.
   - Ⓒ Edwin Hubble repaired it.
   - Ⓓ Astronauts put in a new part.

5. Hubble's pictures help scientists know more about _____.
   - Ⓐ faraway planets
   - Ⓑ diseases
   - Ⓒ underwater life
   - Ⓓ the atmosphere

Bonus: On the back of this page, tell how the Hubble space telescope has helped us learn about space.

Benjamin Franklin

Introducing the Topic

1. Reproduce page 79 for individual students, or make a transparency to use with a group or your whole class.

2. Review the page with students. Help students read the time line and identify important events in Benjamin Franklin's life. Help them to realize his political, humanitarian, and scientific contributions.

Reading the Selections

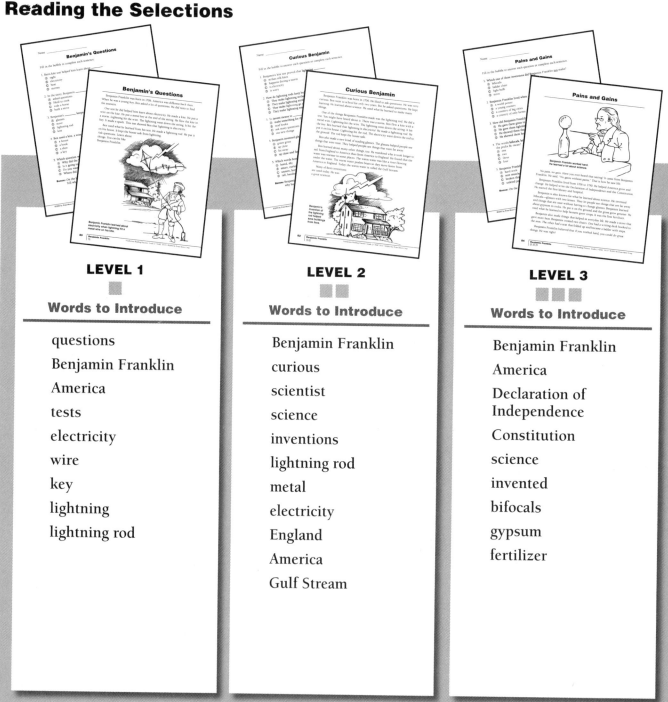

LEVEL 1

Words to Introduce

questions

Benjamin Franklin

America

tests

electricity

wire

key

lightning

lightning rod

LEVEL 2

Words to Introduce

Benjamin Franklin

curious

scientist

science

inventions

lightning rod

metal

electricity

England

America

Gulf Stream

LEVEL 3

Words to Introduce

Benjamin Franklin

America

Declaration of Independence

Constitution

science

invented

bifocals

gypsum

fertilizer

Nonfiction Reading Practice, Grade 2 • EMC 3313 • ©2003 by Evan-Moor Corp.

Time Line of Benjamin Franklin's Life

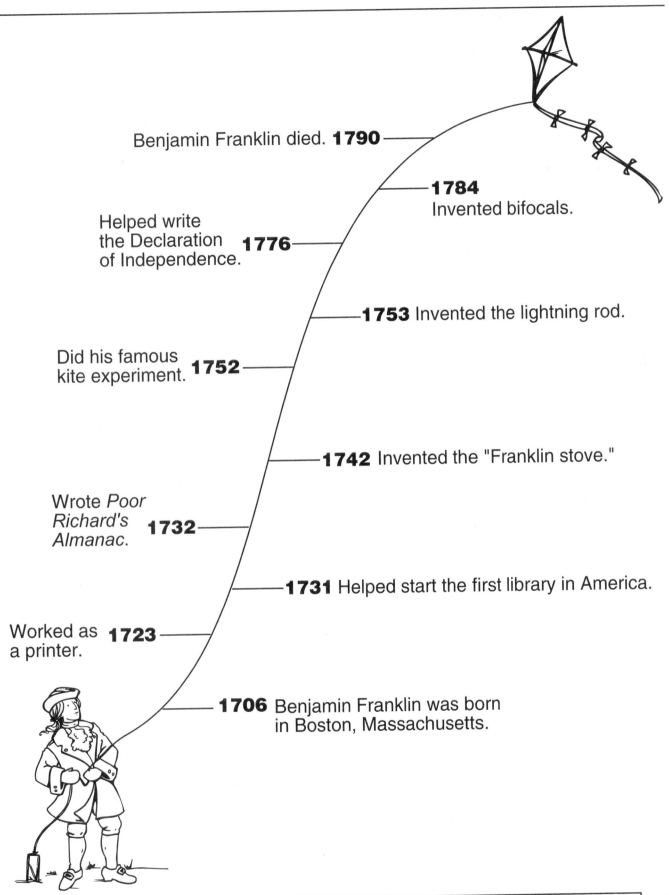

Benjamin Franklin died. **1790**

1784
Invented bifocals.

Helped write
the Declaration
of Independence. **1776**

1753 Invented the lightning rod.

Did his famous
kite experiment. **1752**

1742 Invented the "Franklin stove."

Wrote *Poor
Richard's
Almanac.* **1732**

1731 Helped start the first library in America.

Worked as **1723**
a printer.

1706 Benjamin Franklin was born
in Boston, Massachusetts.

Benjamin's Questions

Benjamin Franklin was born in 1706. America was different back then. When he was a young boy, Ben asked a lot of questions. He did tests to find the answers.

One test he did helped him learn about electricity. He made a kite. He put a wire on the kite. He put a metal key at the end of the string. He flew the kite in a storm. Lightning hit the wire. The lightning went down the string. It hit the key. It made a spark. This test showed Ben that lightning is electricity.

Ben used what he learned from his test. He made a lightning rod. He put it on his house. It kept the house safe from lightning.

Ask questions. Learn about things. You can be like Benjamin Franklin.

Benjamin Franklin learned about electricity when lightning hit a metal wire on his kite.

Nonfiction Reading Practice, Grade 2 • EMC 3313 • ©2003 by Evan-Moor Corp.

Name _____

Benjamin's Questions

Fill in the bubble to complete each sentence.

1. Ben's kite test helped him learn about _____.
   - Ⓐ sight
   - Ⓑ electricity
   - Ⓒ heat
   - Ⓓ storms

2. In the story, Benjamin _____.
   - Ⓐ asked questions
   - Ⓑ liked to cook
   - Ⓒ rode a horse
   - Ⓓ built a stove

3. Benjamin's _____ keeps a home safe during a storm.
   - Ⓐ glasses
   - Ⓑ stove
   - Ⓒ lightning rod
   - Ⓓ kite

4. Ben used a kite, a wire, and _____.
   - Ⓐ a house
   - Ⓑ a book
   - Ⓒ a shoe
   - Ⓓ a key

5. Which question would Benjamin Franklin have asked?
   - Ⓐ Why did the lightning make a spark?
   - Ⓑ Is it going to snow?
   - Ⓒ Do you want to fly a kite?
   - Ⓓ Where did I put my glasses?

Bonus: On the back of this page, draw a picture of Benjamin Franklin's kite. Tell what happened when he flew it during a storm.

Curious Benjamin

Benjamin Franklin was born in 1706. He liked to ask questions. He was very curious. Ben went to school for only two years. But he asked questions. He kept learning. He learned about science. He used what he learned to make many things.

One of the things Benjamin Franklin made was the lightning rod. He did a test. You might have heard about it. There was a storm. Ben flew a kite with a metal wire. Lightning hit the wire. The lightning went down the string. It hit the key. Ben learned that lightning is electricity! He made a lightning rod. He put it on his house. Lightning hit the rod. The electricity went down the rod to the ground. The rod kept the house safe.

Ben also made a new kind of reading glasses. The glasses helped people see things that were near. They helped people see things that were far away.

Ben learned about many other things, too. He wondered why it took longer to sail from England to America than from America to England. He found that the water was warmer in some places. The warm water was like a river flowing under the water. The warm water pushes boats so they move faster from America to England. Today the warm water is called the Gulf Stream.

Many of Ben's inventions are used today. He was a great scientist.

Benjamin's invention of the lightning rod helped save buildings from fires.

Name _____

Curious Benjamin

Fill in the bubble to answer each question or complete each sentence.

1. Benjamin's kite test proved that lightning _____.
   Ⓐ strikes silk kites
   Ⓑ happens during a storm
   Ⓒ is electricity
   Ⓓ is scary

2. How do lightning rods keep buildings safe?
   Ⓐ They make lightning strike far away from the building.
   Ⓑ They make lightning strike the metal in the rod instead of the building.
   Ⓒ They make lightning go through the center of the building.
   Ⓓ They make lightning start fires.

3. To **invent** means to _____.
   Ⓐ make something for the first time
   Ⓑ read books
   Ⓒ ask many questions
   Ⓓ use new things

4. Benjamin invented glasses that helped people see _____.
   Ⓐ green grass
   Ⓑ up close
   Ⓒ far away
   Ⓓ up close and far away

5. Which words best describe Benjamin Franklin?
   Ⓐ bored, shy
   Ⓑ smart, curious
   Ⓒ unsure, lazy
   Ⓓ tall, handsome

Bonus: Benjamin Franklin found the Gulf Stream. On the back of this page, tell why boats go faster when they're in the Gulf Stream.

Pains and Gains

**Benjamin Franklin worked hard.
He learned a lot about science.**

No pain, no gain. Have you ever heard that saying? It came from Benjamin Franklin. He said, "No gains without pains." That is how he saw life.

Benjamin Franklin lived from 1706 to 1790. He helped America grow and change. He helped write the Declaration of Independence and the Constitution. He started the first library and hospital.

Benjamin is also known for what he learned about science. He invented bifocals—glasses with two lenses. They let people see things that are far away and things that are near without having to change glasses. Benjamin learned about gypsum in rocks. He put it on the ground and the grass grew greener. He used what he learned to help farmers grow crops. It was the first fertilizer.

Benjamin also made things that helped in everyday life. He made a stove that gave more heat. Benjamin created two chairs. One had a writing desk hooked to the arm. The other had a seat that folded up and became a ladder with steps.

Benjamin Franklin believed that if you worked hard, you could do great things. He was right!

Pains and Gains

Fill in the bubble to answer each question or complete each sentence.

1. Which one of these inventions did Benjamin Franklin <u>not</u> make?
   - Ⓐ bifocals
   - Ⓑ ladder chair
   - Ⓒ light bulb
   - Ⓓ stove

2. Benjamin Franklin lived when America was _____.
   - Ⓐ a world power
   - Ⓑ a young country
   - Ⓒ a country of big cities
   - Ⓓ a country of only farms

3. How did Benjamin Franklin help farmers grow their crops?
   - Ⓐ He gave them grass to grow.
   - Ⓑ He gave them lightning rods to prevent fires in the fields.
   - Ⓒ He showed them that gypsum could be used as a fertilizer.
   - Ⓓ He showed them how to get rocks out of grass.

4. The words **bifocals**, **binoculars**, and **bicycles** all have the prefix **bi-**. What does the prefix **bi-** mean?
   - Ⓐ one
   - Ⓑ two
   - Ⓒ three
   - Ⓓ four

5. Benjamin Franklin said, "No gains without pains." What **pains** did he mean?
   - Ⓐ hard work
   - Ⓑ sore muscles
   - Ⓒ broken things
   - Ⓓ unkind people

Bonus: On the back of this page, tell about one of Benjamin Franklin's inventions.

Exercise

Introducing the Topic

1. Reproduce page 87 for individual students, or make a transparency to use with a group or your whole class.

2. Have students identify the location. Guide them to notice each form of exercise. Lead them to see that exercise should be fun.

Reading the Selections

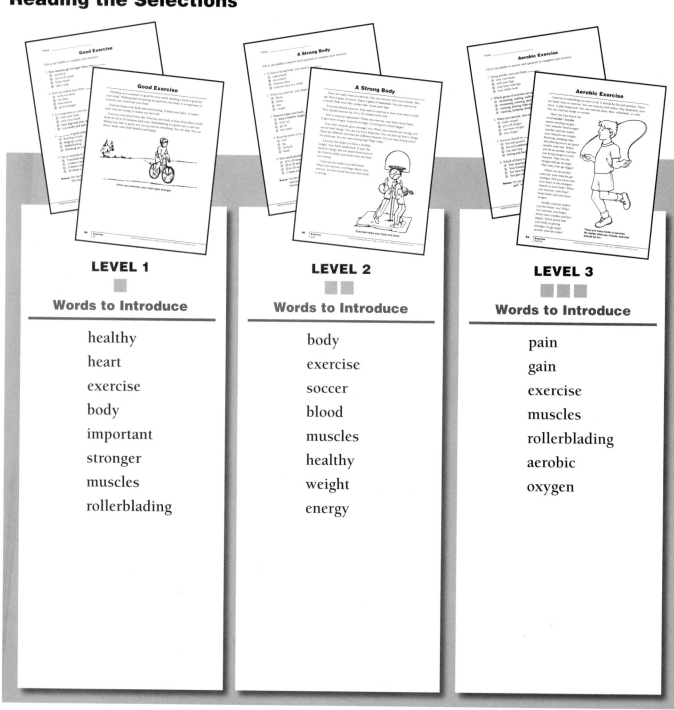

LEVEL 1
■

Words to Introduce

healthy
heart
exercise
body
important
stronger
muscles
rollerblading

LEVEL 2
■ ■

Words to Introduce

body
exercise
soccer
blood
muscles
healthy
weight
energy

LEVEL 3
■ ■ ■

Words to Introduce

pain
gain
exercise
muscles
rollerblading
aerobic
oxygen

Nonfiction Reading Practice, Grade 2 • EMC 3313 • ©2003 by Evan-Moor Corp.

Exercising at the Park

cycling

playing
basketball

jogging

rollerblading

swinging

walking

jumping rope

Good Exercise

Working on a computer is good for your mind. Reading a book is good for your mind. Walking and swimming are good for your body. It is important to exercise your mind and your body.

Exercise keeps your body and mind strong. It helps your heart. It makes other muscles strong. It makes you feel well.

Exercise your mind every day. Exercise your body at least three days a week. Work for 20 to 30 minutes each time. Rollerblading is a good way to exercise. Riding your bike is good, too. Get up and do something. You can skip. You can dance. Make your body healthy and happy.

When you exercise, your heart gets stronger.

Nonfiction Reading Practice, Grade 2 • EMC 3313 • ©2003 by Evan-Moor Corp.

Name _____

Good Exercise

Fill in the bubble to complete each sentence.

1. Your muscles get stronger when you _____.
   - (A) eat lunch
   - (B) run in the park
   - (C) read a book
   - (D) take a nap

2. Exercise makes your heart _____.
   - (A) work too hard
   - (B) not beat
   - (C) beat slower
   - (D) grow stronger

3. It is important to exercise _____.
   - (A) only your body
   - (B) only your mind
   - (C) your legs and your arms
   - (D) your body and your mind

4. _____ is good exercise for your body.
   - (A) Reading a book
   - (B) Singing a song
   - (C) Rollerblading
   - (D) Working on a computer

5. Try to exercise at least _____.
   - (A) 3 seconds each day
   - (B) 2 times a week
   - (C) 3 times a week
   - (D) 20 times a week

Bonus: On the back of this page, tell how you like to exercise. Then tell how the exercise helps your body.

A Strong Body

There are many ways to exercise. You can exercise with your friends. Play tag. Have a game of soccer. Enjoy a game of basketball. You can exercise by yourself. Ride your bike. Jump rope. Swim some laps.

Everyone should exercise. Kids need to exercise at least three days a week. They should exercise for 20 to 30 minutes each time.

Why is exercise important? When you exercise, your heart beats faster. It gets more oxygen. It grows stronger. It even grows a little bigger!

Your other muscles grow stronger, too. When your muscles are strong, you can do hard things. You can run for a long time. You can pick up heavy things. There are different exercises for different muscles. Do you want strong arms? Do push-ups. Do you want strong legs? Ride a bike.

Exercise also helps you have a healthy weight. Your body needs food. It uses the food for energy. But too much food turns to fat. Exercise helps your body turn the food into energy.

Exercise also makes you feel better. When you exercise, you forget about your worries. You feel proud because your body is strong.

Exercise helps your body and mind.

Nonfiction Reading Practice, Grade 2 • EMC 3313 • ©2003 by Evan-Moor Corp.

Name _____

A Strong Body

Fill in the bubble to answer each question or complete each sentence.

1. To have a strong body, you need to _____.
   - Ⓐ read a book
   - Ⓑ eat a snack
   - Ⓒ exercise often
   - Ⓓ exercise once in a while

2. When you exercise, your heart muscle uses more _____.
   - Ⓐ blood
   - Ⓑ bones
   - Ⓒ fats
   - Ⓓ oxygen

3. Exercise helps your body _____.
   - Ⓐ keep a healthy weight
   - Ⓑ wear out
   - Ⓒ get fat
   - Ⓓ stay weak

4. Running makes your _____ muscles stronger.
   - Ⓐ arm
   - Ⓑ leg
   - Ⓒ stomach
   - Ⓓ hand

5. How much should you exercise?
   - Ⓐ 20 to 30 minutes each week
   - Ⓑ 20 to 30 minutes three days a week
   - Ⓒ 20 to 30 minutes each month
   - Ⓓ 3 times a day for 20 to 30 minutes

Bonus: On the back of this page, list three exercises you can do alone and three exercises you can do with your friends. Circle the exercise that is your favorite one to do.

Aerobic Exercise

Exercise is something you have to do. It should be fun and painless. There are many ways to exercise. You can exercise with others. Play basketball, have races, or play hopscotch. You can exercise alone. Bike, rollerblade, or walk. You can exercise inside or outside.

Have you ever heard the word **aerobic**? **Aerobic** means needing oxygen. Your muscles need oxygen. Aerobic exercise makes your muscles use oxygen. Running, jumping rope, and playing soccer are good aerobic exercises. When you do an aerobic exercise, you bring oxygen to your muscles. They use the oxygen and get stronger. They may even get bigger!

When you do aerobic exercise, your muscles get stronger. Did you know that your heart is the strongest muscle in your body? When you exercise, your heart beats faster and uses more oxygen.

Aerobic exercise makes you feel better, too! When you exercise, you forget about your troubles and feel happy. You're proud that your body is getting stronger. So get some aerobic exercise today!

There are many kinds of exercise. No matter which one you choose, exercise should be fun.

Nonfiction Reading Practice, Grade 2 • EMC 3313 • ©2003 by Evan-Moor Corp.

Name _____

Aerobic Exercise

Fill in the bubble to answer each question or complete each sentence.

1. Doing aerobic exercises helps _____.
   - Ⓐ only your heart
   - Ⓑ only your legs
   - Ⓒ your heart and legs
   - Ⓓ your whole body

2. Which group of activities are aerobic exercises?
   - Ⓐ swimming, reading, walking
   - Ⓑ swimming, running, playing tennis
   - Ⓒ running, playing video games, cooking
   - Ⓓ running, jumping, sleeping

3. When you exercise, your muscles _____.
   - Ⓐ make oxygen
   - Ⓑ give off oxygen
   - Ⓒ use more oxygen
   - Ⓓ lose oxygen

4. Exercise should be _____.
   - Ⓐ fun and painful
   - Ⓑ fun and comfortable
   - Ⓒ fast and long
   - Ⓓ boring and hard

5. Which of these is good about exercise?
   - Ⓐ Your muscles get stronger.
   - Ⓑ Your friends don't like you.
   - Ⓒ You have bad dreams.
   - Ⓓ You gain more weight.

Bonus: On the back of this page, tell why people use the phrase "No pain, no gain" when they exercise. Do you think they are correct? Tell why.

Broken Bones

Introducing the Topic

1. Reproduce page 95 for individual students, or make a transparency to use with a group or your whole class.

2. Ask students if they have ever had a broken bone. Show them the skeleton and talk about the different kinds of bones.

Reading the Selections

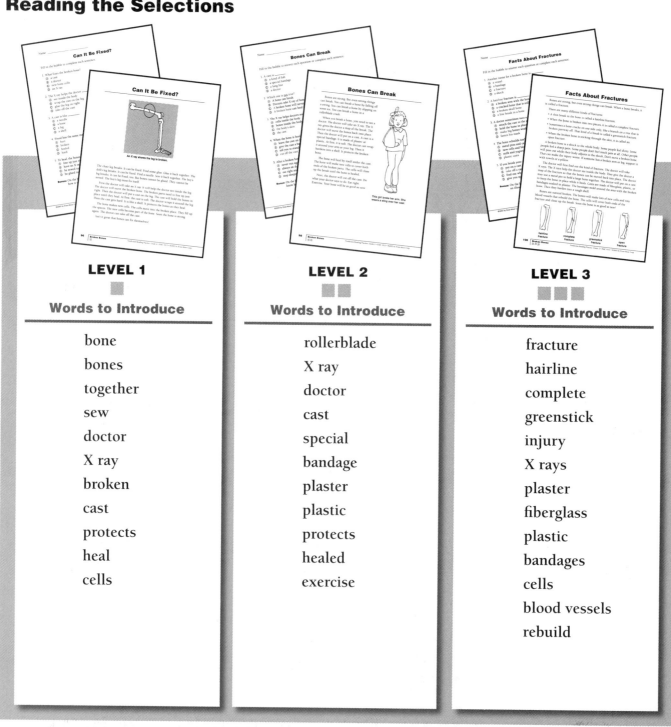

LEVEL 1

Words to Introduce

bone

bones

together

sew

doctor

X ray

broken

cast

protects

heal

cells

LEVEL 2

Words to Introduce

rollerblade

X ray

doctor

cast

special

bandage

plaster

plastic

protects

healed

exercise

LEVEL 3

Words to Introduce

fracture

hairline

complete

greenstick

injury

X rays

plaster

fiberglass

plastic

bandages

cells

blood vessels

rebuild

Your Bones

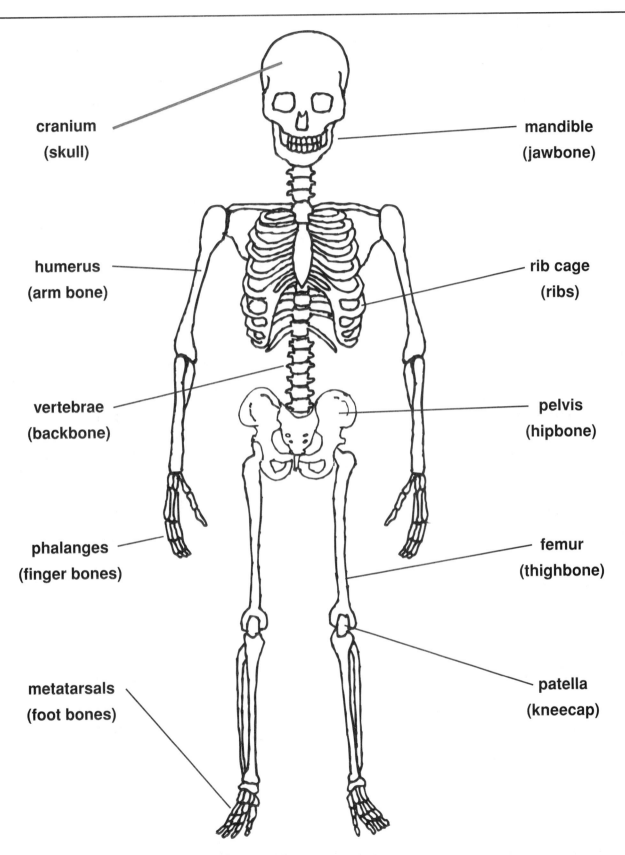

cranium
(skull)

mandible
(jawbone)

humerus
(arm bone)

rib cage
(ribs)

vertebrae
(backbone)

pelvis
(hipbone)

phalanges
(finger bones)

femur
(thighbone)

metatarsals
(foot bones)

patella
(kneecap)

Your bones are strong. But sometimes they can break.

Can It Be Fixed?

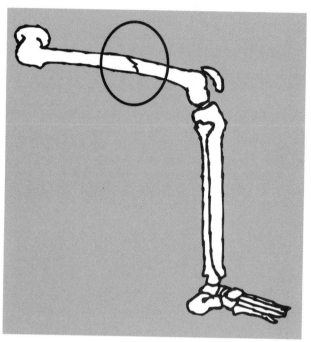

An X ray shows the leg is broken.

The chair leg breaks. It can be fixed. Find some glue. Glue it back together. The doll's leg breaks. It can be fixed. Find a needle. Sew it back together. The boy's leg breaks. It can be fixed, too. But bones cannot be glued. They cannot be sewed. The boy's leg must fix itself.

First the doctor will take an X ray. It will help the doctor see inside the leg. The doctor will move the broken bone. The broken parts need to line up just right. Then the doctor will put a cast on the leg. The cast will hold the bones in place until they heal. At first, the cast is soft. The doctor wraps it around the leg. Then the cast gets hard. It is like a shell. It protects the bones as they heal.

The bone makes new cells. The cells move into the broken place. They fill up the spaces. The new cells become part of the bone. Soon the bone is strong again. The doctor can take off the cast.

Isn't it great that bones can fix themselves!

Nonfiction Reading Practice, Grade 2 • EMC 3313 • ©2003 by Evan-Moor Corp.

Name _____

Can It Be Fixed?

Fill in the bubble to complete each sentence.

1. What fixes the broken bone?
   Ⓐ a cast
   Ⓑ a doctor
   Ⓒ new bone cells
   Ⓓ an X ray

2. The X ray helps the doctor _____.
   Ⓐ see inside the body
   Ⓑ wrap the cast on the leg
   Ⓒ glue the leg on right
   Ⓓ take off the cast

3. A cast is like _____.
   Ⓐ a needle
   Ⓑ a bone
   Ⓒ a leg
   Ⓓ a shell

4. **Fixed** has the same meaning as _____.
   Ⓐ hurt
   Ⓑ broken
   Ⓒ healed
   Ⓓ hard

5. To heal, the bones in the leg need to _____.
   Ⓐ line up just right
   Ⓑ have an X ray
   Ⓒ be sewed together
   Ⓓ be glued together

Bonus: On the back of this page, draw something that was broken. Write about
how it was fixed.

Bones Can Break

Bones are strong. But even strong things can break. You can break a bone by falling off a swing. You can break a bone by slipping on some ice. You can break a bone in a rollerblade crash.

When you break a bone, you need to see a doctor. The doctor will take an X ray. The X ray gives the doctor a map of the break. The doctor will move the bones back into place. Then the doctor will put on a cast. A cast is a special bandage. It is made of plaster or plastic. At first, it is soft. The doctor can wrap it around your arm or your leg. Then it hardens into a shell. It protects the broken bone.

The bone will heal by itself under the cast. The bone will make new cells to cover both ends of the broken parts. The cells will close up the break until the bone is healed.

Next, the doctor will cut off the cast. Do what your doctor says to do. Eat right. Exercise. Your bone will be as good as new.

This girl broke her arm. She wears a sling over her cast.

Nonfiction Reading Practice, Grade 2 • EMC 3313 • ©2003 by Evan-Moor Corp.

Name _____

Bones Can Break

Fill in the bubble to answer each question or complete each sentence.

1. A **cast** is _____.
   - Ⓐ a kind of fish
   - Ⓑ a special bandage
   - Ⓒ a long line
   - Ⓓ a doctor

2. Which one is <u>not</u> true?
   - Ⓐ A bone can break.
   - Ⓑ Doctors take X rays of bones.
   - Ⓒ A broken bone will never heal.
   - Ⓓ A broken bone can heal itself.

3. The X ray helps doctors see _____.
   - Ⓐ cells inside the body
   - Ⓑ bones inside the body
   - Ⓒ the body's skin
   - Ⓓ the cast

4. When the bone is healed, the doctor will _____.
   - Ⓐ leave the cast on for a year
   - Ⓑ give the cast a bath
   - Ⓒ tell you to stand on your head
   - Ⓓ cut off the cast

5. After a broken bone is healed, you should _____.
   - Ⓐ never run again
   - Ⓑ always sit down
   - Ⓒ eat right and exercise
   - Ⓓ stop sleeping

Bonus: On the back of this page, write about a time that you or someone you know had a broken bone.

Facts About Fractures

Bones are strong, but even strong things can break. When a bone breaks, it is called a fracture.

There are many different kinds of fractures:

- A thin break in the bone is called a hairline fracture.

- When the bone is broken into two pieces, it is called a complete fracture.

- Sometimes a bone cracks on one side only, like a branch on a tree that is broken partway off. That kind of a break is called a greenstick fracture.

- When the broken bone is sticking through the skin, it is called an open fracture.

A broken bone is a shock to the whole body. Some people feel dizzy. Some people feel a sharp pain. Some people don't feel much pain at all. Other people will pass out while their body adjusts to the shock. Don't move a broken bone. That can make the injury worse. If someone has a broken arm or leg, support it with towels or a pillow.

The doctor will first find out the kind of fracture. The doctor will take X rays. The X rays help the doctor see inside the body. They give the doctor a map of the fracture so that the bones can be moved back into place. The doctor may use a metal pin to hold a large bone together. The doctor will put on a cast to keep the bone in place while it heals. Casts are made of fiberglass, plastic, or bandages soaked in plaster. The bandages mold around the area with the broken bone. Then they harden into a tough shell.

Bones are natural healers. The bones will make lots of new cells and tiny blood vessels that rebuild the bone. The cells will cover both ends of the fracture and close up the break. Soon the bone is as good as new!

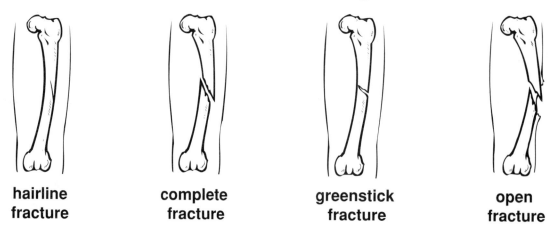

| hairline fracture | complete fracture | greenstick fracture | open fracture |

Name _____

Facts About Fractures

Fill in the bubble to answer each question or complete each sentence.

1. Another name for a broken bone is _____.
   - Ⓐ a vessel
   - Ⓑ a bandage
   - Ⓒ a fracture
   - Ⓓ a shock

2. A **hairline fracture** is _____.
   - Ⓐ a broken arm with the bone sticking out of the skin
   - Ⓑ a cracked bone that is still partly attached
   - Ⓒ a broken skull bone
   - Ⓓ a line break in a bone

3. A doctor sometimes uses a metal pin to _____.
   - Ⓐ attach the cast to the arm
   - Ⓑ hold the bone in place until it heals
   - Ⓒ make big bones weaker
   - Ⓓ fasten his mask

4. The bone rebuilds itself with _____.
   - Ⓐ metal pins and calcium
   - Ⓑ new cells and blood vessels
   - Ⓒ milk and yogurt
   - Ⓓ plastic casts

5. If you break your arm, the first thing the doctor will do is _____.
   - Ⓐ put on a cast
   - Ⓑ take off a cast
   - Ⓒ find out what kind of fracture it is
   - Ⓓ give you special exercises to do

Bonus: On the back of this page, list the different kinds of fractures and draw an illustration that shows each one.

Clara Barton

Introducing the Topic

1. Reproduce page 103 for individual students, or make a transparency to use with a group or your whole class.

2. Help students read the time line and identify major events in Clara Barton's life.

Reading the Selections

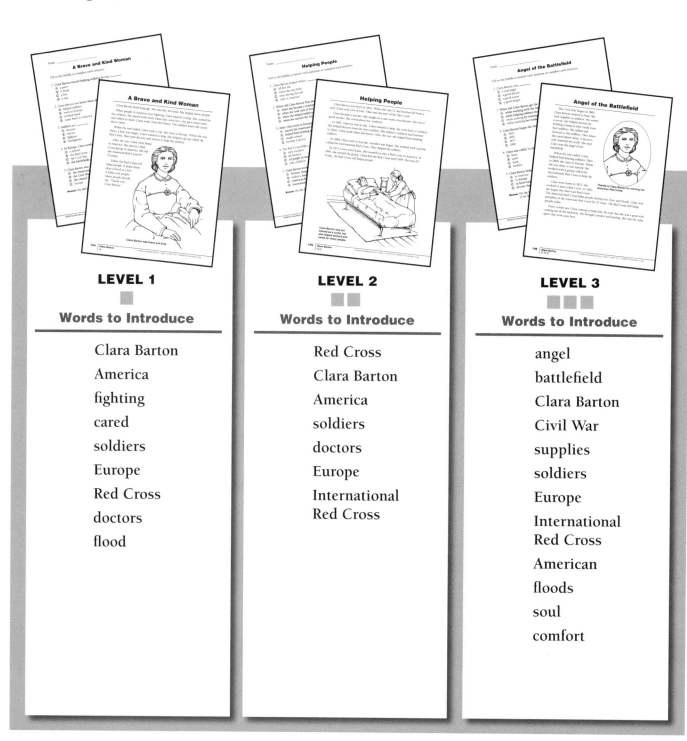

LEVEL 1

Words to Introduce

Clara Barton
America
fighting
cared
soldiers
Europe
Red Cross
doctors
flood

LEVEL 2

Words to Introduce

Red Cross
Clara Barton
America
soldiers
doctors
Europe
International
Red Cross

LEVEL 3

Words to Introduce

angel
battlefield
Clara Barton
Civil War
supplies
soldiers
Europe
International
Red Cross
American
floods
soul
comfort

Nonfiction Reading Practice, Grade 2 • EMC 3313 • ©2003 by Evan-Moor Corp.

Time Line of Clara Barton's Life

Clara Barton lived from 1821 to 1912. We remember her kindness and bravery.

1821 — Clara Barton was born.

1836 — Began teaching.

1861 — Helped soldiers during the Civil War.

1870 — Helped the International Red Cross.

1881 — Began the American Red Cross.

1904 — Wrote *A Story of the Red Cross.*

1912 — Clara Barton died.

A Brave and Kind Woman

Clara Barton lived long ago. She was shy, but kind. She helped many people.

When people in America were fighting, Clara wanted to help. She cooked for the soldiers. She stayed with them when they were hurt. She gave them water and talked to them. Clara made them feel better. The soldiers knew she cared about them.

When the war ended, Clara took a trip. She went to Europe. While she was there, a new war began. Clara wanted to help. She helped a group called the Red Cross. They sent doctors and nurses to help the soldiers.

After the war, Clara went home to America. She started a Red Cross group in America. She led the American Red Cross for 23 years.

Today, the Red Cross still helps people. It helps them after a flood or a fire. It helps sick people. Many people should say, "Thank you, Clara Barton."

Clara Barton was brave and kind.

Nonfiction Reading Practice, Grade 2 • EMC 3313 • ©2003 by Evan-Moor Corp.

Name _____

A Brave and Kind Woman

Fill in the bubble to complete each sentence.

1. Clara Barton started helping soldiers during _____.
   - Ⓐ a party
   - Ⓑ a flood
   - Ⓒ a fire
   - Ⓓ a war

2. Clara Barton was brave when she _____.
   - Ⓐ helped soldiers
   - Ⓑ went to Europe
   - Ⓒ worked hard
   - Ⓓ came back to America

3. **Soldiers** are _____.
   - Ⓐ doctors
   - Ⓑ nurses
   - Ⓒ fighters
   - Ⓓ firefighters

4. In Europe, Clara worked with _____.
   - Ⓐ a school
   - Ⓑ the Red Cross
   - Ⓒ the Civil War
   - Ⓓ the battlefields

5. Clara Barton was president of _____.
   - Ⓐ the American Red Cross
   - Ⓑ the Civil War
   - Ⓒ the United States
   - Ⓓ Europe

Bonus: On the back of this page, tell one reason why we say Clara Barton was kind.

Helping People

Clara Barton was born in 1821. When she was 11, her brother fell from a roof. Clara took care of him. That was the start of her life's work.

Clara became a teacher. She taught in a one-room schoolhouse. She was a good teacher. She cared about her students.

In 1861, America was at war. Clara wanted to help. She took food to soldiers. She helped doctors treat the hurt soldiers. She talked to the soldiers and listened to them. Clara made them feel better. After the war, she helped find missing soldiers.

In 1869, Clara went to Europe. Another war began. She worked with a group called the International Red Cross. They helped the soldiers.

In 1873, Clara went home. She wanted to start a Red Cross in America. In 1881, she started the group. Clara led the Red Cross until 1904. She was 83. Today, the Red Cross still helps people.

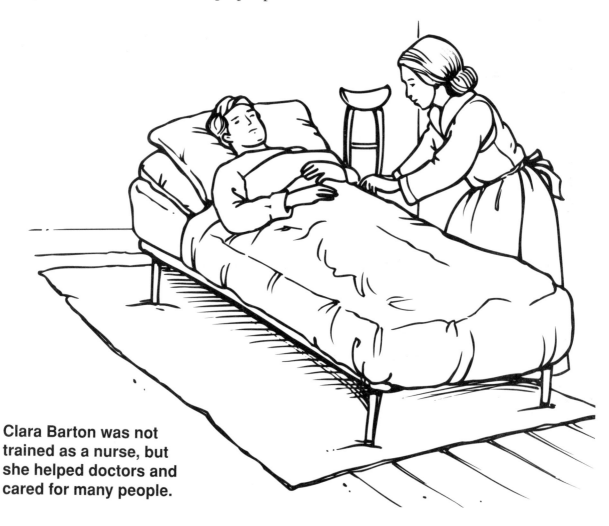

Clara Barton was not trained as a nurse, but she helped doctors and cared for many people.

Nonfiction Reading Practice, Grade 2 • EMC 3313 • ©2003 by Evan-Moor Corp.

Name _____

Helping People

Fill in the bubble to answer each question or complete each sentence.

1. Clara Barton helped others _____.
   - Ⓐ all her life
   - Ⓑ when she was little
   - Ⓒ only during the war
   - Ⓓ only in America

2. When did Clara Barton first show that she wanted to help other people?
   - Ⓐ when she became a teacher
   - Ⓑ when she took care of her brother
   - Ⓒ when she helped soldiers in the Civil War
   - Ⓓ when she started the American Red Cross

3. After Clara went to Europe, she _____.
   - Ⓐ started the American Red Cross
   - Ⓑ helped find missing soldiers
   - Ⓒ taught school
   - Ⓓ became a doctor

4. The Red Cross helps _____.
   - Ⓐ only truckers
   - Ⓑ all farmers
   - Ⓒ all people in need
   - Ⓓ only children

5. Clara Barton worked with the _____. She wanted a _____ in America.
   - Ⓐ doctors, hospital
   - Ⓑ soldiers, battlefield
   - Ⓒ American Red Cross, war
   - Ⓓ International Red Cross, Red Cross

Bonus: On the back of this page, tell one way the American Red Cross helps people.

Angel of the Battlefield

The Civil War began in 1861. Clara Barton wanted to help. She took supplies to soldiers. She wasn't a nurse. She helped doctors by holding a lamp so they could treat hurt soldiers. She talked and listened to the soldiers. They knew she cared about them. A doctor's wife watched her work. She said Clara was the angel of the battlefield.

When the war ended, Clara helped find missing soldiers. Then in 1869, she went to Europe. While she was there, a war started. She worked with a group called the International Red Cross to help the soldiers.

Thanks to Clara Barton for starting the American Red Cross.

Clara went home in 1873. She worked to start a Red Cross. In 1881, she began the American Red Cross. The American Red Cross helps people during war, fires, and floods. Clara was president of the American Red Cross for 23 years. The Red Cross still helps people today.

Once, a man saw Clara coming to help him. He said that she was a great soul coming out of the darkness. She brought comfort and healing. She was the calm spirit that took away fear.

Nonfiction Reading Practice, Grade 2 • EMC 3313 • ©2003 by Evan-Moor Corp.

Name _____

Angel of the Battlefield

Fill in the bubble to answer each question or complete each sentence.

1. Clara Barton was _____.
   - Ⓐ a real angel
   - Ⓑ a good doctor
   - Ⓒ a good nurse
   - Ⓓ a good helper

2. When did Clara Barton get the idea for the American Red Cross?
   - Ⓐ while working with the International Red Cross in Europe
   - Ⓑ while helping soldiers during the Civil War
   - Ⓒ while looking for missing soldiers in America
   - Ⓓ while teaching her students

3. Clara Barton began the American Red Cross in _____.
   - Ⓐ 1821
   - Ⓑ 1861
   - Ⓒ 1873
   - Ⓓ 1881

4. Clara was called "a calm spirit." **Calm** means _____.
   - Ⓐ busy
   - Ⓑ quiet
   - Ⓒ kind
   - Ⓓ healthy

5. Clara Barton helped soldiers _____.
   - Ⓐ in America
   - Ⓑ in Europe
   - Ⓒ in both America and Europe
   - Ⓓ all over the world

Bonus: On the back of this page, tell why Clara Barton was known as the angel of the battlefield.

Estimating Cost

Introducing the Topic

1. Reproduce page 111 for individual students, or make a transparency to use with a group or your whole class.

2. Present the number line to students. Help them use it to gain practice with rounding to the nearest dollar.

Reading the Selections

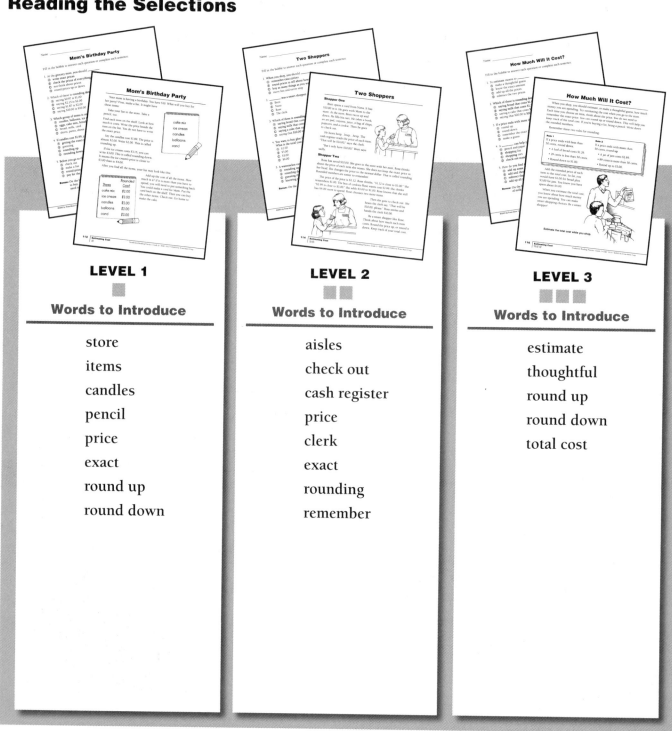

LEVEL 1

Words to Introduce

store

items

candles

pencil

price

exact

round up

round down

LEVEL 2

Words to Introduce

aisles

check out

cash register

price

clerk

exact

rounding

remember

LEVEL 3

Words to Introduce

estimate

thoughtful

round up

round down

total cost

Rounding Numbers

If the number is **1**, **2**, **3**, or **4**, round **down**.

If the number is **5**, **6**, **7**, **8**, or **9**, round **up**.

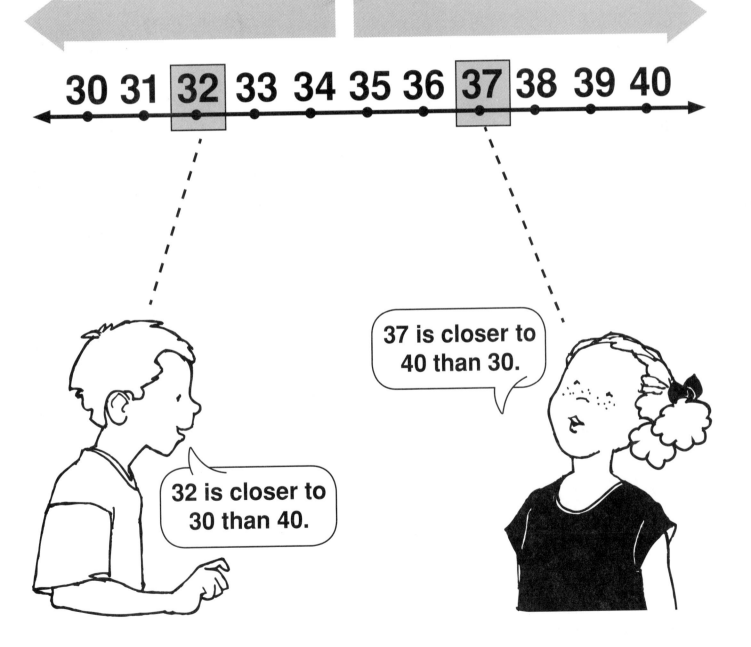

37 is closer to 40 than 30.

32 is closer to 30 than 40.

Mom's Birthday Party

Your mom is having a birthday. You have $10. What will you buy for her party? First, make a list. It might have the items listed on the pad:

Take your list to the store. Take a pencil, too. Find each item on the shelf. Look at how much it costs. Write the price beside the item on the list. You do not have to write the exact price.

cake mix
ice cream
candles
balloons
card

Say the candles cost $1.99. The price is almost $2.00. Write $2.00. This is called rounding up.

If the ice cream costs $3.15, you can write $3.00. This is called rounding down. It means the ice cream's price is closer to $3.00 than to $4.00.

After you find all the items, your list may look like this:

Items	Rounded Cost
cake mix	$2.00
ice cream	$3.00
candles	$2.00
balloons	$2.00
card	$3.00

Add up the cost of all the items. How much is it? If it is more than you have to spend, you will need to put something back. You could make a card for Mom. Put the card back on the shelf. Then you can buy the other items. Check out. Go home to make the cake.

Nonfiction Reading Practice, Grade 2 • EMC 3313 • ©2003 by Evan-Moor Corp.

Name _____

Mom's Birthday Party

Fill in the bubble to answer each question or complete each sentence.

1. At the grocery store, you should _____.
   - Ⓐ write exact prices
   - Ⓑ check the prices of everything in the store
   - Ⓒ not think about prices
   - Ⓓ round prices up or down

2. Which of these is **rounding down**?
   - Ⓐ saying $0.97 is $1.00
   - Ⓑ saying $2.15 is $2.00
   - Ⓒ saying $1.87 is $2.00
   - Ⓓ saying $10.00 is $10.00

3. Which group of items is on the list?
   - Ⓐ candles, balloons, ice cream
   - Ⓑ eggs, cake mix, bread
   - Ⓒ bread, milk, card
   - Ⓓ shirts, pants, shoes

4. If candles cost $1.99, you can write $2.00. This is called _____.
   - Ⓐ getting the exact price
   - Ⓑ guessing
   - Ⓒ rounding up
   - Ⓓ rounding down

5. Before you go to the grocery store, you should _____.
   - Ⓐ check out
   - Ⓑ make a list
   - Ⓒ round prices up or down
   - Ⓓ pay for the items

Bonus: On the back of this page, tell the name of something you would like to buy. Then tell about how much it costs and how much money you need to buy it.

Two Shoppers

Shopper One

Brett opens a card from Nana. It has $10.00 in it. He goes with Mom to the store. At the store, Brett races up and down. He fills his cart. He takes a book, an art pad, crayons, juice, a bag of chips, popcorn, and a cookie. Then he goes to check out.

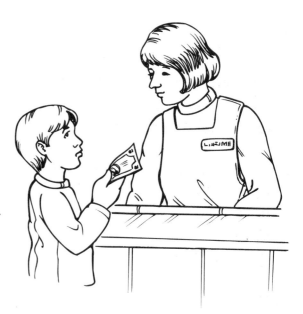

He hears beep…beep…beep. The cash register reads the price of each item. "That will be $14.00," says the clerk.

"But I only have $10.00," Brett says sadly.

Shopper Two

Rose has saved $10.00. She goes to the store with her aunt. Rose thinks about the price of each item she wants. She does not keep the exact price in her head. She changes the price to the nearest dollar. That is called rounding. Rounded numbers are easier to remember.

The price of the juice is $1.12. Rose thinks, "$1.12 is close to $1.00." She remembers $1.00. The box of cookies Rose wants costs $2.99. She thinks "$2.99 is close to $3.00." She adds $3.00 to $1.00. Rose knows that she still has $6.00 more to spend. Rose chooses two more items.

Then she goes to check out. She hears the clerk say, "That will be $10.00, please." Rose smiles and hands the clerk $10.00.

Be a smart shopper like Rose. Think about how much each item costs. Round the price up, or round it down. Keep track of your total cost.

Nonfiction Reading Practice, Grade 2 • EMC 3313 • ©2003 by Evan-Moor Corp.

Name _____

Two Shoppers

Fill in the bubble to answer each question or complete each sentence.

1. When you shop, you should _____.
   - Ⓐ remember exact prices
   - Ⓑ round prices to tell about how much things cost
   - Ⓒ buy as many things as you want
   - Ⓓ move fast and never stop

2. _____ was a smart shopper.
   - Ⓐ Brett
   - Ⓑ Nana
   - Ⓒ Rose
   - Ⓓ The clerk

3. Which of these is **rounding up**?
   - Ⓐ saying bread that costs $1.99 is about $2.00
   - Ⓑ saying milk that costs $1.25 is about $1.00
   - Ⓒ saying a cake that costs $2.05 is about $2.00
   - Ⓓ saying that $10.00 is $10.00

4. You want to buy glue for $2.00, markers for $3.00, and paper for $1.00. What is the total cost of these items?
   - Ⓐ $2.00
   - Ⓑ $3.00
   - Ⓒ $5.00
   - Ⓓ $6.00

5. A watermelon costs $3.05. You can say it costs about $3.00. This is _____.
   - Ⓐ rounding up
   - Ⓑ rounding down
   - Ⓒ guessing the price
   - Ⓓ knowing the exact price

Bonus: On the back of this page, tell what you can do to be a smart shopper.

How Much Will It Cost?

When you shop, you should estimate, or make a thoughtful guess, how much money you are spending. Try estimating the cost when you go to the store. Each time you choose an item, think about the price. You do not need to remember the exact price. You can round up or round down. This will help you keep track of the total cost. If you're buying a lot, bring a pencil. Write down the rounded numbers.

Remember these two rules for rounding:

Rule 1	**Rule 2**
If a price ends with **less** than 50 cents, round **down**.	If a price ends with **more** than 50 cents, round **up**.
• A loaf of bread costs $1.29.	• A jar of jam costs $2.89.
• 29 cents is less than 50 cents.	• 89 cents is more than 50 cents.
• Round down to $1.00.	• Round up to $3.00.

Add the rounded price of each item to the total cost. So far, you would have $1.00 for bread plus $3.00 for jam. You know you have spent about $4.00.

When you estimate the total cost, you know about how much money you are spending. You can make smart shopping choices. Be a smart shopper!

Estimate the total cost while you shop.

Nonfiction Reading Practice, Grade 2 • EMC 3313 • ©2003 by Evan-Moor Corp.

Name _____

How Much Will It Cost?

Fill in the bubble to answer each question or complete each sentence.

1. To **estimate** means to _____.
   - Ⓐ make a thoughtful guess
   - Ⓑ know the exact amount
   - Ⓒ add up all the prices
   - Ⓓ subtract the two prices

2. Which of these is **rounding down?**
   - Ⓐ saying bread that costs $1.99 is about $2.00
   - Ⓑ saying milk that costs $1.25 is about $1.00
   - Ⓒ saying a cake that costs $2.85 is about $3.00
   - Ⓓ saying that $20.00 is $20.00

3. If a price ends with more than 50¢, you should _____.
   - Ⓐ round up
   - Ⓑ round down
   - Ⓒ remember the exact price
   - Ⓓ make a guess

4. A _____ can help you remember the cost of the rounded price.
   - Ⓐ pencil and paper
   - Ⓑ shopping list
   - Ⓒ shopping cart
   - Ⓓ check-out stand

5. How do you find the total cost of the items?
   - Ⓐ add up some of the items
   - Ⓑ add and then subtract
   - Ⓒ subtract the total cost
   - Ⓓ add up all the items

Bonus: On the back of this page, explain the rule for rounding up. Use the price of milk, $1.89, as an example.

Fractions

Introducing the Topic

1. Reproduce page 119 for individual students, or make a transparency to use with a group or your whole class.

2. Explain the different fractional representations. Have students identify the number of equal parts used in each fraction.

Reading the Selections

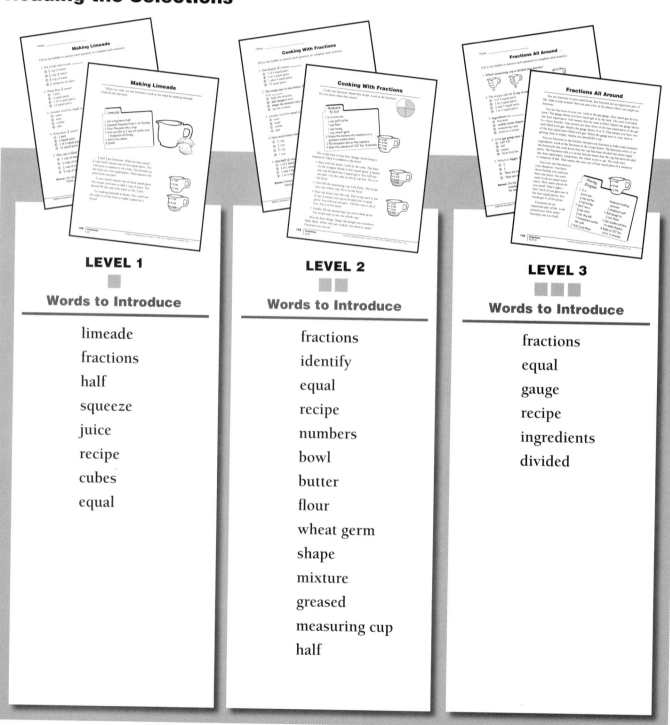

LEVEL 1
■

Words to Introduce

limeade

fractions

half

squeeze

juice

recipe

cubes

equal

LEVEL 2
■ ■

Words to Introduce

fractions

identify

equal

recipe

numbers

bowl

butter

flour

wheat germ

shape

mixture

greased

measuring cup

half

LEVEL 3
■ ■ ■

Words to Introduce

fractions

equal

gauge

recipe

ingredients

divided

Nonfiction Reading Practice, Grade 2 • EMC 3313 • ©2003 by Evan-Moor Corp.

Fractions

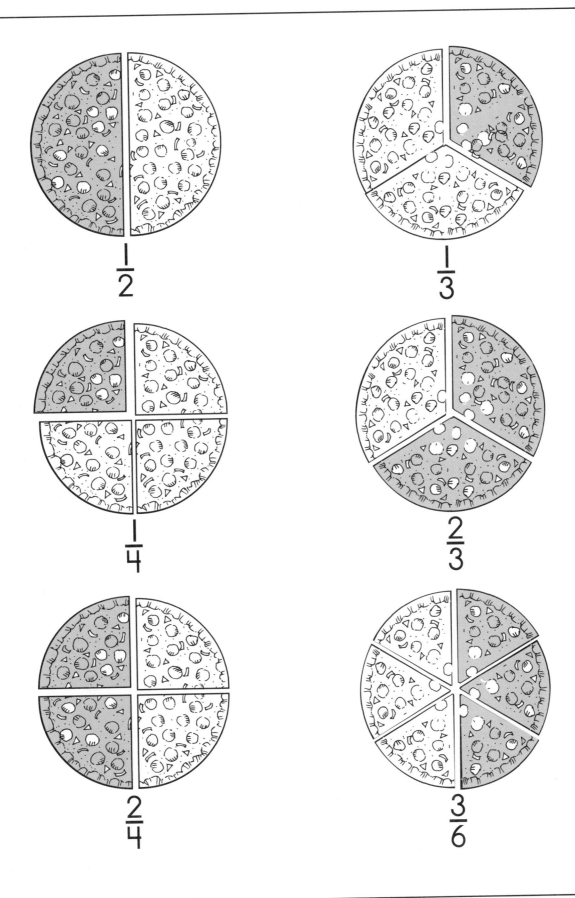

$$\frac{1}{2}$$

$$\frac{1}{3}$$

$$\frac{1}{4}$$

$$\frac{2}{3}$$

$$\frac{2}{4}$$

$$\frac{3}{6}$$

Making Limeade

When we cook, we use fractions. Look at the steps for making limeade. Find all the fractions.

Limeade

1. Cut a big lime in half.
2. Squeeze the juice from $\frac{1}{2}$ of the lime.
3. Pour the juice into a cup.
4. Add and stir in $\frac{1}{3}$ cup of water and 1 teaspoon of honey.
5. Add 2 ice cubes.
6. Drink!

$\frac{1}{2}$ and $\frac{1}{3}$ are fractions. What do they mean? $\frac{1}{2}$ (one-half) means one of two equal parts. The card says to squeeze $\frac{1}{2}$ of a lime. You should cut the lime into two equal parts. Then squeeze the juice from one part.

$\frac{1}{3}$ (one-third) means one of three equal parts. The recipe card says to add $\frac{1}{3}$ cup of water. You should fill the cup with water to the $\frac{1}{3}$ line.

Try making limeade at home. You could use the other $\frac{1}{2}$ of the lime to make a glass for a friend.

Nonfiction Reading Practice, Grade 2 • EMC 3313 • ©2003 by Evan-Moor Corp.

Name _____

Making Limeade

Fill in the bubble to answer each question or complete each sentence.

1. The recipe says to use _____.
   - Ⓐ $\frac{1}{2}$ cup of water
   - Ⓑ $\frac{1}{3}$ cup of water
   - Ⓒ $\frac{2}{3}$ cup of water
   - Ⓓ $\frac{1}{3}$ teaspoon of water

2. What does $\frac{1}{2}$ mean?
   - Ⓐ 1 part
   - Ⓑ 2 equal parts
   - Ⓒ 1 of 2 equal parts
   - Ⓓ 12 equal parts

3. Another word for **equal** is _____.
   - Ⓐ same
   - Ⓑ near
   - Ⓒ unlike
   - Ⓓ add

4. What does $\frac{1}{3}$ mean?
   - Ⓐ 1 part
   - Ⓑ 3 equal parts
   - Ⓒ 1 of 3 equal parts
   - Ⓓ 13 equal parts

5. This cup is filled with _____.
   - Ⓐ 1 cup of water
   - Ⓑ 2 cups of water
   - Ⓒ $\frac{1}{3}$ cup of water
   - Ⓓ $\frac{2}{3}$ cup of water

Bonus: On the back of this page, write one of the fractions from the recipe.
Draw a picture to show the fraction.

Cooking with Fractions

Cooks use fractions. Read this recipe. Look at the fractions. Do you know what they mean?

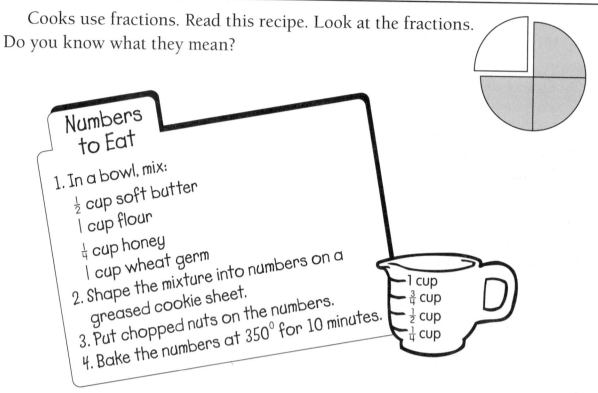

Numbers to Eat

1. In a bowl, mix:
   - $\frac{1}{2}$ cup soft butter
   - 1 cup flour
   - $\frac{1}{4}$ cup honey
   - 1 cup wheat germ
2. Shape the mixture into numbers on a greased cookie sheet.
3. Put chopped nuts on the numbers.
4. Bake the numbers at 350° for 10 minutes.

The recipe says to mix four things. Each thing is measured. Then it is added to the bowl.

- Start with the butter. Look at the cube. The lines on the wrapper divide it into equal parts. $\frac{1}{2}$ means one cup divided into 2 equal parts. You will use one part. Cut the cube on the $\frac{1}{2}$ cup line. Put it in the bowl.

- Next, fill the measuring cup with flour. The recipe says one whole cup. Put it in the bowl.

- Pour the honey into the cup. The recipe says to use $\frac{1}{4}$ cup. $\frac{1}{4}$ means one cup is divided into 4 equal parts. You will use one part. Fill the cup to the $\frac{1}{4}$ line. Put it in the bowl.

- Finally, fill the measuring cup with wheat germ. The recipe says to use one whole cup.

Mix the four things. Shape the dough into numbers. Bake them. When they are cooked, use them to make fractions you can eat.

Nonfiction Reading Practice, Grade 2 • EMC 3313 • ©2003 by Evan-Moor Corp.

Cooking with Fractions

Fill in the bubble to answer each question or complete each sentence.

1. **One-fourth** ($\frac{1}{4}$) means _____.
   - Ⓐ 1 of 4 equal parts
   - Ⓑ 4 of 1 equal parts
   - Ⓒ 1 plus 4 equal parts
   - Ⓓ 14 equal parts

2. The recipe says to mix butter, flour, honey, and wheat germ. The next step is to _____.
   - Ⓐ bake the mixture
   - Ⓑ add chopped nuts
   - Ⓒ shape the mixture into numbers
   - Ⓓ eat the cookies

3. Another word for **equal** is _____.
   - Ⓐ near
   - Ⓑ same
   - Ⓒ unlike
   - Ⓓ add

4. How much honey does the recipe say to use?
   - Ⓐ $\frac{1}{2}$ cup
   - Ⓑ $\frac{1}{4}$ cup
   - Ⓒ $\frac{3}{4}$ cup
   - Ⓓ 1 cup

5. **One-half** ($\frac{1}{2}$) means _____.
   - Ⓐ 1 of 2 equal parts
   - Ⓑ 2 of 1 equal parts
   - Ⓒ 1 and 2 equal parts
   - Ⓓ 1 or 2 equal parts

Bonus: Pretend you followed the recipe. On the back of this page, draw a cookie fraction. Tell what it means.

Fractions All Around

You see fractions in your math book. But fractions are an important part of life. Take a look around. Here are just a few of the places where you might see fractions.

You see fractions in your car. Look at the gas gauge. How much gas do you have? The gauge shows you how much gas is in the tank. The tank is divided into four equal parts. **Full** means that the tank is filled. Maybe the gauge shows ¾—three-fourths. That means you have three of the four equal parts of the gas tank filled with gas. Maybe the gauge shows ½ or ²⁄₄. That means you have two of the four equal parts filled with gas. When the gauge says ¼, your tank is getting close to empty. Maybe you should fill it up.

You see fractions in the kitchen. Recipes use fractions to help cooks measure ingredients. Look at the fractions in the recipe below. The fractions with a 3 on the bottom let the cook know that the cup has been divided into three equal parts. The fractions with a 4 on the bottom mean that the cup has been divided into four equal parts. Sometimes, the whole is not a cup. The cook uses ¼ teaspoon of salt. That means she uses one of four equal parts of a teaspoon.

You even use fractions at your sleepover. You have three friends over and you have one pizza. You each want to eat an equal-sized piece. How many pieces do you need? That's right—four. Each of you gets one of the four equal pieces. You would get ¼ of the pizza.

Fractions are an important part of life. Look around you. How many fractions can you find?

Honey Shapes

1. In a bowl, mix:
   $\frac{1}{3}$ cup butter
   $\frac{1}{4}$ cup honey
2. Next, mix in
   $\frac{2}{3}$ cup oats
   $\frac{1}{3}$ cup dry milk
   4 teaspoons water
   Mix well.
3. Add $\frac{1}{3}$ cup flour

1 cup
$\frac{2}{3}$ cup
$\frac{1}{3}$ cup

1 teaspoon baking powder
$\frac{1}{4}$ teaspoon salt
4. Roll dough to $\frac{1}{4}$ inch thick.
5. Use cookie cutters to make shapes.
6. Bake at 325° for 10 to 15 minutes.

Nonfiction Reading Practice, Grade 2 • EMC 3313 • ©2003 by Evan-Moor Corp.

Name _____

Fractions All Around

Fill in the bubble to answer each question or complete each sentence.

1. Which measuring cup is divided into **fourths**?

   Ⓐ   Ⓑ   Ⓒ   Ⓓ

2. The recipe calls for $\frac{2}{3}$ cup of oats. What does $\frac{2}{3}$ mean?
   - Ⓐ 2 of 3 equal parts
   - Ⓑ 3 of 2 equal parts
   - Ⓒ 2 and 3 equal parts
   - Ⓓ 2 or 3 equal parts

3. **Ingredients** are _____.
   - Ⓐ fractions
   - Ⓑ cookie-cutter shapes
   - Ⓒ measuring cups
   - Ⓓ items in a recipe

4. If the gas gauge says $\frac{1}{4}$, the tank is getting close to _____.
   - Ⓐ half full
   - Ⓑ full
   - Ⓒ empty
   - Ⓓ three-fourths

5. Which is bigger, $\frac{1}{4}$ or $\frac{1}{2}$?
   - Ⓐ $\frac{1}{4}$
   - Ⓑ $\frac{1}{2}$
   - Ⓒ They are equal.
   - Ⓓ They are not equal.

Bonus: On the back of this page, write two fractions from the recipe. Use a circle, measuring cup, or other picture to show the number of equal parts used for each fraction.

Metric Measurements

Introducing the Topic

1. Reproduce page 127 for individual students, or make a transparency to use with a group or your whole class.

2. Show students the metric ruler. Point out millimeters and centimeters. Have students answer the questions. If possible, have them use a real metric ruler and paper clip to compare.

Reading the Selections

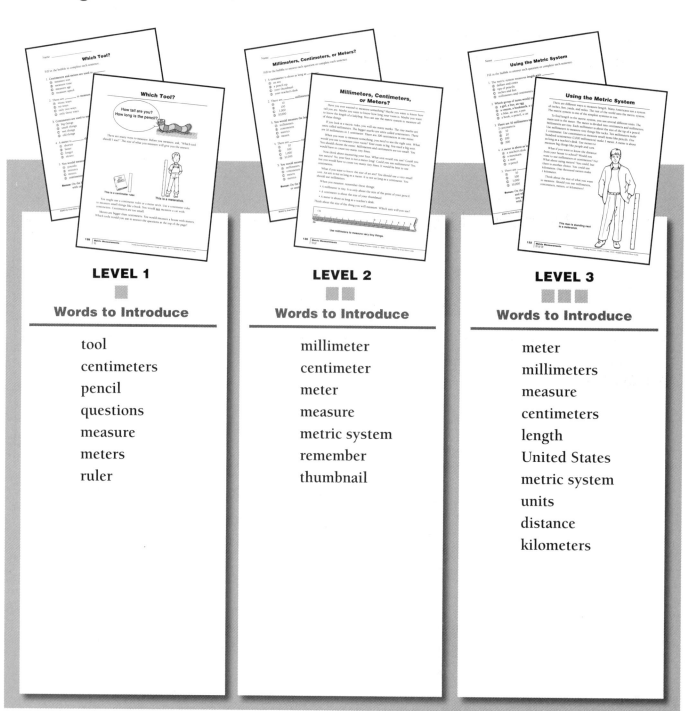

LEVEL 1
■

Words to Introduce

tool

centimeters

pencil

questions

measure

meters

ruler

LEVEL 2
■ ■

Words to Introduce

millimeter

centimeter

meter

measure

metric system

remember

thumbnail

LEVEL 3
■ ■ ■

Words to Introduce

meter

millimeters

measure

centimeters

length

United States

metric system

units

distance

kilometers

Nonfiction Reading Practice, Grade 2 • EMC 3313 • ©2003 by Evan-Moor Corp.

A Metric Ruler

A metric ruler can show millimeters, centimeters, and a meter. This ruler shows millimeters and centimeters.

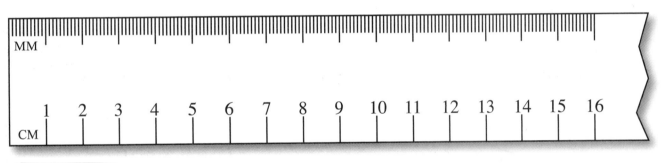

How many centimeters is one paper clip?

How many centimeters is two paper clips?

Which Tool?

How tall are you?
How long is the pencil?

There are many ways to measure. Before you measure, ask, "Which tool should I use?" The size of what you measure will give you the answer.

This is a centimeter ruler.

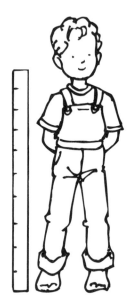

This is a meterstick.

You might use a centimeter ruler or a meterstick. Use a centimeter ruler to measure small things like a book. You would <u>not</u> measure a car with centimeters. Centimeters are too small.

Meters are bigger than centimeters. You would measure a house with meters. Which tools would you use to answer the questions at the top of the page?

Nonfiction Reading Practice, Grade 2 • EMC 3313 • ©2003 by Evan-Moor Corp.

Name _____

Which Tool?

Fill in the bubble to complete each sentence.

1. Centimeters and meters are used to _____.
   - Ⓐ measure size
   - Ⓑ measure time
   - Ⓒ measure age
   - Ⓓ measure speed

2. There are _____ to measure things.
   - Ⓐ many ways
   - Ⓑ no ways
   - Ⓒ only two ways
   - Ⓓ only three ways

3. Centimeters are used to measure _____.
   - Ⓐ big things
   - Ⓑ small things
   - Ⓒ wet things
   - Ⓓ old things

4. A **meter** is _____ than a centimeter.
   - Ⓐ shorter
   - Ⓑ faster
   - Ⓒ longer
   - Ⓓ slower

5. You would measure a pencil with _____.
   - Ⓐ pounds
   - Ⓑ minutes
   - Ⓒ meters
   - Ⓓ centimeters

Bonus: On the back of this page, tell the name of something you would measure with centimeters and something you would measure with meters.

Millimeters, Centimeters, or Meters?

Have you ever wanted to measure something? Maybe you want to know how tall you are. Maybe you want to know how long your room is. Maybe you want to know the length of a ladybug. You can use the metric system to measure all of these things.

If you look at a metric ruler, you will see many marks. The tiny marks are units called millimeters. The bigger marks are units called centimeters. There are 10 millimeters in 1 centimeter. There are 100 centimeters in one meter.

When you want to measure something, you need to use the right unit. What would you use to measure your room? Your room is big. You need a big unit. You should choose the meter. Millimeters and centimeters are too small. You would have to count too many tiny lines.

Now think about measuring your foot. What unit would you use? Could you use meters? No, your foot is not a meter long! Could you use millimeters? Yes, but you would have to count too many tiny lines. It would be best to use centimeters.

What if you want to know the size of an ant? You should use a very small unit. An ant is not as long as a meter. It is not as long as a centimeter. You should use millimeters.

When you measure, remember these things:

- A millimeter is tiny. It is only about the size of the point of your pencil.

- A centimeter is about the size of your thumbnail.

- A meter is about as long as a teacher's desk.

Think about the size of the thing you will measure. Which unit will you use?

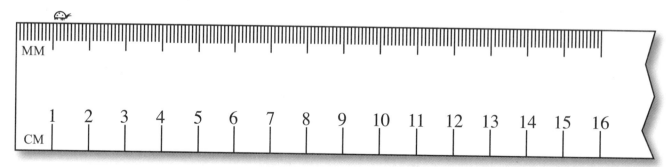

Use millimeters to measure very tiny things.

Name _____

Millimeters, Centimeters, or Meters?

Fill in the bubble to answer each question or complete each sentence.

1. A **centimeter** is about as long as _____.
   - Ⓐ an ant
   - Ⓑ a pencil tip
   - Ⓒ your thumbnail
   - Ⓓ your teacher's desk

2. There are _____ millimeters in 1 centimeter.
   - Ⓐ 10
   - Ⓑ 100
   - Ⓒ 1,000
   - Ⓓ 10,000

3. You would measure the length of a car with _____.
   - Ⓐ millimeters
   - Ⓑ centimeters
   - Ⓒ metrics
   - Ⓓ meters

4. There are _____ centimeters in 1 meter.
   - Ⓐ 10
   - Ⓑ 100
   - Ⓒ 1,000
   - Ⓓ 10,000

5. You would measure the length of a pencil with _____.
   - Ⓐ millimeters
   - Ⓑ centimeters
   - Ⓒ meters
   - Ⓓ metrics

Bonus: On the back of this page, tell why you should use meters, <u>not</u> millimeters or centimeters, to measure the length of your room.

Using the Metric System

There are different ways to measure length. Many Americans use a system of inches, feet, yards, and miles. The rest of the world uses the metric system. The metric system is one of the simplest systems to use.

To find length in the metric system, you use several different units. The main unit is the meter. The meter is divided into centimeters and millimeters. Millimeters are tiny. Each millimeter is about the size of the tip of a pencil. Use millimeters to measure tiny things like tacks. Ten millimeters make 1 centimeter. Use centimeters to measure small items like pencils. One hundred centimeters (1,000 millimeters) make 1 meter. A meter is about as long as a teacher's desk. Use meters to measure big things like people and cars.

What if you want to know the distance from your house to school? Would you want to use millimeters or centimeters? No! What about using meters? You could, but there is another choice. You could use kilometers. One thousand meters make 1 kilometer.

Think about the size of what you want to measure. Should you use millimeters, centimeters, meters, or kilometers?

This man is standing next to a meterstick.

Nonfiction Reading Practice, Grade 2 • EMC 3313 • ©2003 by Evan-Moor Corp.

Name _____

Using the Metric System

Fill in the bubble to answer each question or complete each sentence.

1. The metric system measures length with _____.
   - Ⓐ dollars and cents
   - Ⓑ tips of pencils
   - Ⓒ inches and feet
   - Ⓓ millimeters and centimeters

2. Which group of items would you measure with **centimeters**?
   - Ⓐ a girl, a bus, an egg
   - Ⓑ a crayon, a bookmark, a cat
   - Ⓒ a bike, an ant, a pea
   - Ⓓ a book, a pencil, a car

3. There are 10 millimeters in 1 centimeter. There are _____ millimeters in 2 centimeters.
   - Ⓐ 10
   - Ⓑ 20
   - Ⓒ 100
   - Ⓓ 200

4. A **meter** is about as long as _____.
   - Ⓐ a teacher's desk
   - Ⓑ a mountain
   - Ⓒ a man
   - Ⓓ a pencil

5. There are _____ meters in 1 kilometer.
   - Ⓐ 10
   - Ⓑ 100
   - Ⓒ 1,000
   - Ⓓ 10,000

Bonus: On the back of this page, tell when you would measure with meters and when you would measure with kilometers. Then name something you would measure with millimeters and something you would measure with centimeters.

Work Songs

Introducing the Topic

1. Reproduce page 135 for individual students, or make a transparency to use with a group or your whole class.

2. Share with students that work songs are familiar tunes that help us remember our history. Songs were sung to lift people's spirits as they worked. We still sing these songs today.

Reading the Selections

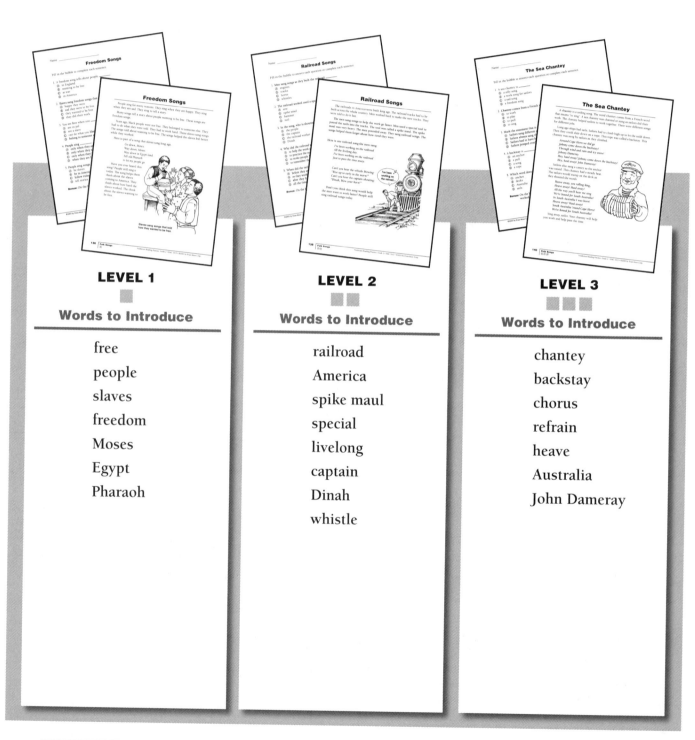

LEVEL 1	LEVEL 2	LEVEL 3
Words to Introduce	**Words to Introduce**	**Words to Introduce**
free	railroad	chantey
people	America	backstay
slaves	spike maul	chorus
freedom	special	refrain
Moses	livelong	heave
Egypt	captain	Australia
Pharaoh	Dinah	John Dameray
	whistle	

Work Songs

Sing a Song While You Work

Freedom Songs
Slaves sang songs about wanting to be free.

Railroad Songs
Workers sang songs to make the work go faster.

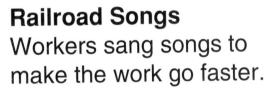

Sea Chanteys
Sailors sang songs while they worked on the ship.

Freedom Songs

People sing for many reasons. They sing when they are happy. They sing when they are sad. They sing to tell a story.

Many songs tell a story about people wanting to be free. These songs are freedom songs.

Years ago, black people were not free. They belonged to someone else. They had to do what they were told. They had to work hard. These slaves sang songs. The songs told about wanting to be free. The songs helped the slaves feel better while they worked.

Here is part of a song that slaves sang long ago.

Go down, Moses.
Way down in Egypt land.
Tell old Pharaoh
to let my people go.

Have you ever heard this song? People still sing it today. The song helps them think about the slaves coming to America. They think about how hard the slaves worked. They think about the slaves wanting to be free.

Slaves sang songs that told how they wanted to be free.

Nonfiction Reading Practice, Grade 2 • EMC 3313 • ©2003 by Evan-Moor Corp.

Name _____

Freedom Songs

Fill in the bubble to complete each sentence.

1. A freedom song tells about people _____.
   - Ⓐ in England
   - Ⓑ wanting to be free
   - Ⓒ at war
   - Ⓓ in America

2. Slaves sang freedom songs that told how _____.
   - Ⓐ happy they were
   - Ⓑ sad they were to be free
   - Ⓒ they wanted to be free
   - Ⓓ they did their work

3. You are **free** when you _____.
   - Ⓐ are in jail
   - Ⓑ are a slave
   - Ⓒ can do what you like
   - Ⓓ belong to someone else

4. People sing _____.
   - Ⓐ only when they are sad
   - Ⓑ only when they are glad
   - Ⓒ only when they want something
   - Ⓓ when they are happy or sad

5. People sing songs so they can _____.
   - Ⓐ be slaves
   - Ⓑ be in America
   - Ⓒ follow rules
   - Ⓓ tell stories

Bonus: On the back of this page, tell something you like to sing about.

Railroad Songs

The railroads in America were built long ago. The railroad tracks had to be built across the whole country. Men worked hard to make the new tracks. They were told to do it fast.

The men sang songs to help the work go faster. Men used a special tool to pound the nails into the tracks. The tool was called a spike maul. The spike maul was very heavy. The men pounded away. They sang railroad songs. The songs helped them forget about how tired they were.

Here is one railroad song the men sang.

I've been working on the railroad
All the livelong day.
I've been working on the railroad
Just to pass the time away.

Can't you hear the whistle blowing:
"Rise up so early in the morn!"
Can't you hear the captain shouting:
"Dinah, blow your horn!"

Don't you think this song would help the men want to work faster? People still sing railroad songs today.

Nonfiction Reading Practice, Grade 2 • EMC 3313 • ©2003 by Evan-Moor Corp.

Name _____

Railroad Songs

Fill in the bubble to answer each question or complete each sentence.

1. Men sang songs as they built the railroad _____.
   - Ⓐ engines
   - Ⓑ tracks
   - Ⓒ horns
   - Ⓓ whistles

2. The railroad worker used a special tool called _____.
   - Ⓐ a saw
   - Ⓑ a hammer
   - Ⓒ a spike maul
   - Ⓓ a nail

3. In the song, who is shouting on the train?
   - Ⓐ the people
   - Ⓑ the captain
   - Ⓒ the railroad worker
   - Ⓓ Dinah

4. Why did the railroad workers sing?
   - Ⓐ to help the work go faster
   - Ⓑ to practice the songs
   - Ⓒ to make people laugh
   - Ⓓ to remember the words

5. When did the railroad workers sing?
   - Ⓐ before they ate
   - Ⓑ all the time
   - Ⓒ after they finished
   - Ⓓ as they worked

Bonus: On the back of this page, write about a song you sing while you work.

The Sea Chantey

A chantey is a sailing song. The word **chantey** comes from a French word that means "to sing." A sea chantey was chanted, or sung, as sailors did their work. The chantey helped sailors to work together. There were different songs for different jobs.

Long ago, ships had sails. Sailors had to climb high up to let the sails down. Then they could slide down on a rope. This rope was called a backstay. This chantey was sung by sailors as they climbed.

Around Cape Horn we did go
Johnny come down the backstay!
Through wind and rain and icy snow!
Johnny Dameray.
Hey, haul away! Johnny come down the backstay!
Hey, haul away! John Dameray!

Sailors also sang a chantey as the anchor was raised. This chantey had a steady beat. The sailors would stamp on the deck as they shouted the words.

Heave away, you rolling king,
Heave away! Haul away!
All the way you'll hear me sing
We're bound for South Australia!
In South Australia I was born!
Heave away! Haul away!
South Australia 'round Cape Horn!
We're bound for South Australia!

Sing away, sailor. Your chantey will help you work and help pass the time.

Nonfiction Reading Practice, Grade 2 • EMC 3313 • ©2003 by Evan-Moor Corp.

Name _____

The Sea Chantey

Fill in the bubble to answer each question or complete each sentence.

1. A **sea chantey** is _____.
   - Ⓐ a silly song
   - Ⓑ a work song for sailors
   - Ⓒ a sad song
   - Ⓓ a freedom song

2. **Chantey** comes from a French word that means _____.
   - Ⓐ to work
   - Ⓑ to play
   - Ⓒ to pull
   - Ⓓ to sing

3. Mark the statement that is true.
   - Ⓐ Sailors sang different songs for different jobs.
   - Ⓑ Sailors always sang the songs all alone.
   - Ⓒ Sailors had to have beautiful voices.
   - Ⓓ Sailors jumped overboard when they finished singing.

4. A **backstay** is _____.
   - Ⓐ an anchor
   - Ⓑ a pull
   - Ⓒ a song
   - Ⓓ a rope

5. Which word does <u>not</u> belong? _____.
   - Ⓐ anchor
   - Ⓑ decks
   - Ⓒ Australia
   - Ⓓ sails

Bonus: On the back of this page, write two reasons why sailors sang as they worked.

Photography

Introducing the Topic

1. Reproduce page 143 for individual students, or make a transparency to use with a group or your whole class.

2. Ask students if they have ever used a camera. Show students the picture of the camera and read and discuss the labels.

Reading the Selections

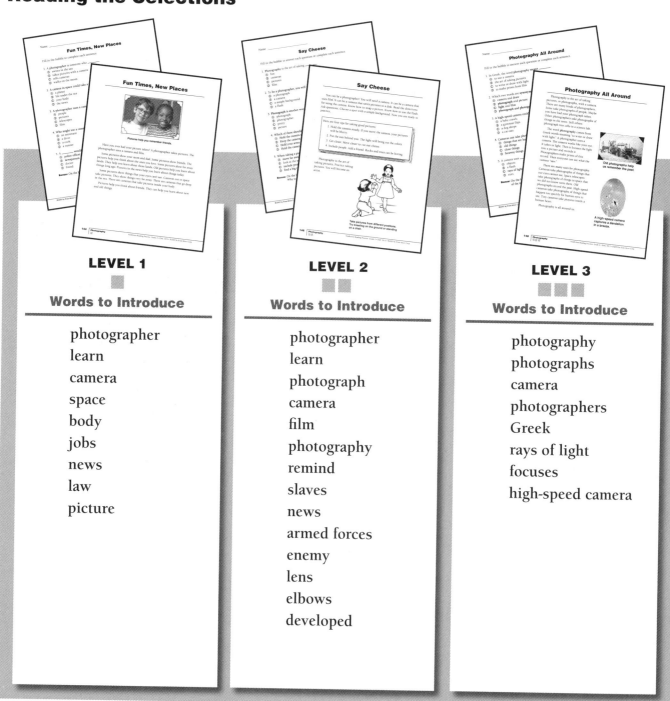

LEVEL 1

Words to Introduce

photographer
learn
camera
space
body
jobs
news
law
picture

LEVEL 2

Words to Introduce

photographer
learn
photograph
camera
film
photography
remind
slaves
news
armed forces
enemy
lens
elbows
developed

LEVEL 3

Words to Introduce

photography
photographs
camera
photographers
Greek
rays of light
focuses
high-speed camera

Parts of a Camera

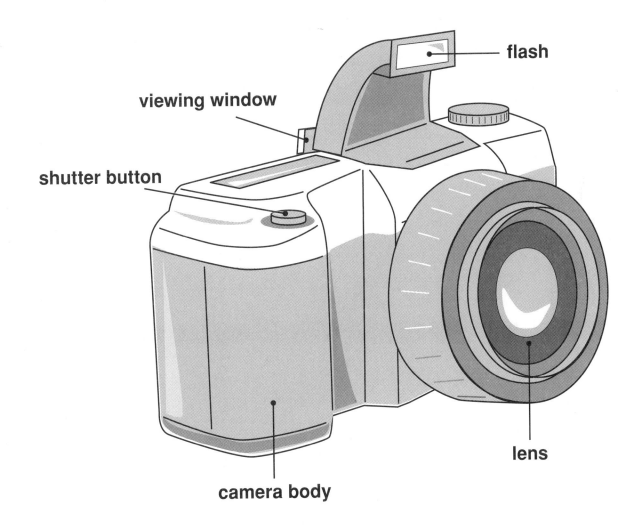

flash

viewing window

shutter button

lens

camera body

Fun Times, New Places

Pictures help you remember friends.

Have you ever had your picture taken? A photographer takes pictures. The photographer uses a camera and film.

Some pictures show your mom and dad. Some pictures show friends. The pictures help you think about the ones you love. Some pictures show faraway lands. They help you learn about those lands. Old pictures help you learn about things long ago. Pictures in the news help you learn about things today.

Some pictures show things that your eyes can't see. Cameras out in space take pictures. They show things very far away. There are cameras that go deep in the sea. There are cameras that take pictures inside your body.

Pictures help you think about friends. They can help you learn about new and old things.

Nonfiction Reading Practice, Grade 2 • EMC 3313 • ©2003 by Evan-Moor Corp.

Name _____

Fun Times, New Places

Fill in the bubble to complete each sentence.

1. A **photographer** is someone who _____.
   - Ⓐ swims in the sea
   - Ⓑ takes pictures with a camera
   - Ⓒ sells cameras
   - Ⓓ walks on the moon

2. A camera in space could take a picture of _____.
   - Ⓐ a planet
   - Ⓑ life under the sea
   - Ⓒ your body
   - Ⓓ the news

3. A photographer uses a camera and _____.
   - Ⓐ people
   - Ⓑ pictures
   - Ⓒ telescopes
   - Ⓓ film

4. Who might use a camera underwater? _____.
   - Ⓐ an astronaut
   - Ⓑ a diver
   - Ⓒ a cook
   - Ⓓ a runner

5. A _____ would use photographs of small things in your body.
   - Ⓐ police officer
   - Ⓑ newsperson
   - Ⓒ doctor
   - Ⓓ friend

Bonus: On the back of this page, tell about a time you had your picture taken.

Say Cheese

You can be a photographer! You will need a camera. It can be a camera that uses film. It can be a camera that saves pictures to a disk. Read the directions for using the camera. Know how to snap a picture. Know how to use the flash. Ask questions. Choose a spot with a simple background. Now you are ready to practice.

Here are four tips for taking good pictures:

1. Hold the camera steady. If you move the camera, your pictures will be blurry.

2. Put the sun behind you. The light will bring out the colors.

3. Get closer. Move closer to cut out clutter.

4. Include people. Add a friend. Rocks and trees can be boring.

Photography is the art of taking pictures. Practice taking pictures. You will become an artist.

Take pictures from different positions. Try kneeling on the ground or standing on a chair.

Nonfiction Reading Practice, Grade 2 • EMC 3313 • ©2003 by Evan-Moor Corp.

Name _____

Say Cheese

Fill in the bubble to answer each question or complete each sentence.

1. **Photography** is the art of taking _____.
   - (A) fun
   - (B) cameras
   - (C) pictures
   - (D) film

2. To be a photographer, you will need _____.
   - (A) a photograph
   - (B) a camera
   - (C) a simple background
   - (D) a flash

3. **Photograph** is another word for _____.
   - (A) photograph
   - (B) photographer
   - (C) pretty
   - (D) picture

4. Which of these should you remember when you use a camera?
   - (A) Hold the camera steady.
   - (B) Keep the camera shaky.
   - (C) Hold your arms above your body.
   - (D) Hold the camera the same way every time.

5. When taking a picture, it is a good idea to _____.
   - (A) move far away
   - (B) look at the sun
   - (C) include people
   - (D) find a big rock

Bonus: On the back of this page, describe your favorite photograph. What is it of? Why is it your favorite? Why was the photograph taken?

Photography All Around

Photography is the art of taking pictures, or photographs, with a camera. There are many kinds of photographers. Some take photographs of people. Maybe you have had your photograph taken. Other photographers take photographs of things in the news. Still others photograph tiny cells in a science lab.

The word **photography** comes from Greek words meaning "to write or draw with light." A photographer uses a camera. The camera works like your eye. It takes in light. Then it focuses the light into a picture and records it. Photographers make prints of this record. Then everyone can see what the camera "saw."

Old photographs help us remember the past.

There are many uses for photography. Cameras take photographs of things that our eyes cannot see. Space telescopes take photographs of things in space that we did not know were there. Old photographs record the past. High-speed cameras take photographs of things that happen too quickly for human eyes to see. Tiny cameras take pictures inside a human heart.

Photography is all around us.

A high-speed camera captures a dandelion in a breeze.

Nonfiction Reading Practice, Grade 2 • EMC 3313 • ©2003 by Evan-Moor Corp.

Name _____

Photography All Around

Fill in the bubble to answer each question or complete each sentence.

1. In Greek, the word **photography** means _____.
   - Ⓐ to use a camera
   - Ⓑ the art of taking pictures
   - Ⓒ to write or draw with light
   - Ⓓ to make prints from film

2. Which two words are **synonyms**?
   - Ⓐ **camera** and **draw**
   - Ⓑ **photograph** and **picture**
   - Ⓒ **light** and **film**
   - Ⓓ **photograph** and **photographer**

3. A high-speed camera could show us how _____.
   - Ⓐ a baby crawls
   - Ⓑ a gymnast flips
   - Ⓒ a dog sleeps
   - Ⓓ a cat eats

4. Cameras can take photographs only of _____.
   - Ⓐ things that are happening now
   - Ⓑ old things
   - Ⓒ close things
   - Ⓓ faraway things

5. A camera uses _____ to "draw" a picture.
   - Ⓐ objects
   - Ⓑ a flash
   - Ⓒ rays of light
   - Ⓓ eyes

Bonus: On the back of this page, explain why doctors would like to have pictures of the inside of the heart.

Old-Time Radio

Introducing the Topic

1. Reproduce page 151 for individual students, or make a transparency to use with a group or your whole class.

2. Present the illustration to students. Help them understand that the old-time radio series were broadcast live. Guide them to understand the limitations of the performers. Help them understand the profound impact that the radio shows had in terms of family entertainment.

Reading the Selections

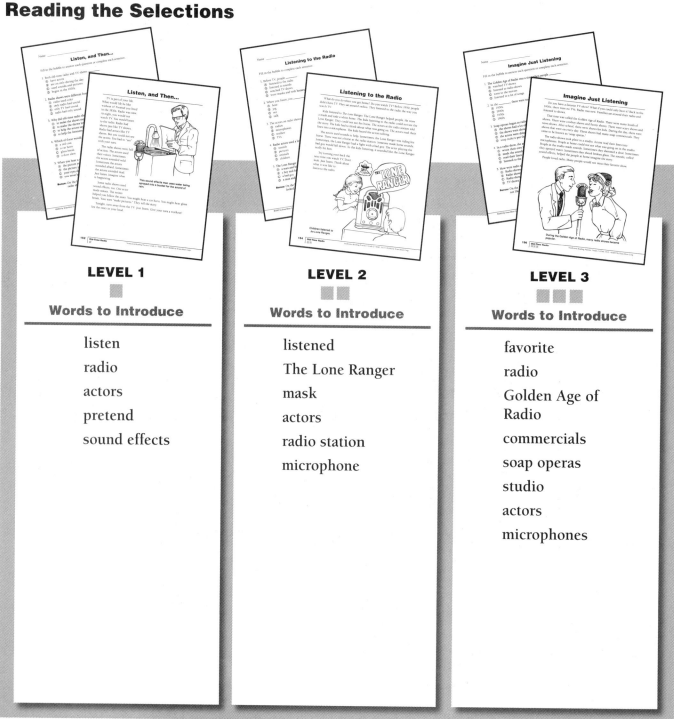

LEVEL 1

Words to Introduce

listen

radio

actors

pretend

sound effects

LEVEL 2

Words to Introduce

listened

The Lone Ranger

mask

actors

radio station

microphone

LEVEL 3

Words to Introduce

favorite

radio

Golden Age of Radio

commercials

soap operas

studio

actors

microphones

Nonfiction Reading Practice, Grade 2 • EMC 3313 • ©2003 by Evan-Moor Corp.

Old-Time Radio

Families listened to radio programs.

Listen, and Then...

TV is part of your life. What would life be like without it? Pretend you lived in the 1930s. Radio was new. At night, you would not watch TV. You would listen to the radio. Radio had shows just like TV shows. Radio had actors like TV shows. But you could not see the actors. You had to "see" with your ears.

The radio shows were full of action. The actors used their voices. Sometimes the actors sounded wild. Sometimes the actors sounded afraid. Sometimes the actors sounded mad. Just listen. Imagine what is happening.

This sound effects man uses water being sprayed into a bucket for the sound of rain.

Some radio shows used sound effects, too. One actor made noises. The noises helped you follow the story. You might hear a car horn. You might hear glass break. Your ears "make pictures." They tell the story.

Tonight, turn away from the TV. Just listen. Give your ears a workout! See the story in your head.

Name _____

Listen, and Then...

Fill in the bubble to answer each question or complete each sentence.

1. Both old-time radio and TV shows _____.
   - Ⓐ have actors
   - Ⓑ are on only during the day
   - Ⓒ used sounds and pictures
   - Ⓓ began in the 1930s

2. Radio shows were different from TV because _____.
   - Ⓐ radio used color
   - Ⓑ only radio had sound
   - Ⓒ only TV had sound
   - Ⓓ radio had only sound

3. Why did old-time radio shows use sound effects?
   - Ⓐ to make the shows more like TV
   - Ⓑ to make the shows loud
   - Ⓒ to help the actors say their lines
   - Ⓓ to help the listeners imagine the story

4. Which of these would you <u>not</u> hear?
   - Ⓐ a red coat
   - Ⓑ a car horn
   - Ⓒ glass break
   - Ⓓ a door slam

5. When you hear a radio show, _____.
   - Ⓐ the picture your mind makes will be the same as everyone else's
   - Ⓑ the picture your mind makes will be your own
   - Ⓒ your eyes do all the work
   - Ⓓ you must be standing up

Bonus: On the back of this page, tell what it was like to listen to an old-time radio show. Would you like it? Why or why not?

Listening to the Radio

What do you do when you get home? Do you watch TV? Before 1950, people didn't have TV. They sat around radios. They listened to the radio the way you watch TV.

Kids listened to *The Lone Ranger.* The Lone Ranger helped people. He wore a mask and rode a white horse. The kids listening to the radio could not see the Lone Ranger. They could not see his horse. The actors at the radio station told the story. The kids had to think about what was going on. The actors read their lines into a microphone. The kids heard the actors talking.

The actors used sounds to help. Sometimes, the Lone Ranger was riding his horse. There was not a horse at the radio station. Someone made horse sounds. Sometimes, the Lone Ranger had a fight with a bad guy. The actor playing the bad guy would fall down. To the kids listening, it sounded like the Lone Ranger really hit him.

Try turning your back the next time you watch TV. Don't look. Just listen. Think about what it was like to listen to the radio.

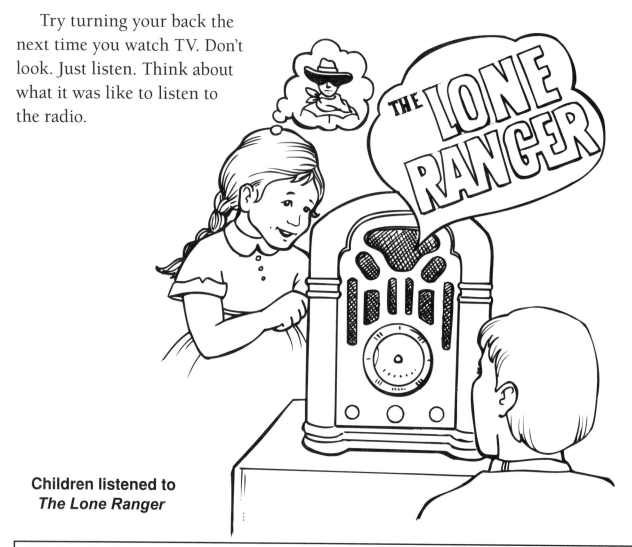

Children listened to
The Lone Ranger

Nonfiction Reading Practice, Grade 2 • EMC 3313 • ©2003 by Evan-Moor Corp.

Name _____

Listening to the Radio

Fill in the bubble to complete each sentence.

1. Before TV, people _____.
   - Ⓐ listened to the radio
   - Ⓑ listened to sounds
   - Ⓒ watched TV shows
   - Ⓓ wore masks and rode horses

2. When you listen, you _____.
   - Ⓐ hear
   - Ⓑ jog
   - Ⓒ see
   - Ⓓ talk

3. The actors on radio shows had to speak into _____.
   - Ⓐ radios
   - Ⓑ microphones
   - Ⓒ studios
   - Ⓓ TVs

4. Radio actors used a lot of _____.
   - Ⓐ sounds
   - Ⓑ pictures
   - Ⓒ animals
   - Ⓓ children

5. The Lone Ranger was about _____.
   - Ⓐ a man and his horse
   - Ⓑ a boy and his dog
   - Ⓒ a bad guy
   - Ⓓ a man and a boat

Bonus: On the back of this page, draw what you think the Lone Ranger looked like.

Imagine Just Listening

Do you have a favorite TV show? What if you could only hear it? Back in the 1930s, there were no TVs. Radio was new. Families sat around their radio and listened to shows.

That time was called the Golden Age of Radio. There were many kinds of shows. There were cowboy shows and funny shows. There were scary shows and news shows. After school, there were shows for kids. During the day, there were shows that were on every day. These shows had many soap commercials. They came to be known as "soap operas."

The radio shows took place in a studio. Actors read their lines into microphones. People at home could not see what was going on in the studio. People in the studio made sounds. Sometimes they slammed a door. Sometimes they sprayed water. Sometimes they shook broken glass. The sounds, called sound effects, helped the people at home imagine the story.

People loved radio. Many people would not miss their favorite show.

During the Golden Age of Radio, many radio shows became popular.

Nonfiction Reading Practice, Grade 2 • EMC 3313 • ©2003 by Evan-Moor Corp.

Imagine Just Listening

Fill in the bubble to answer each question or complete each sentence.

1. The Golden Age of Radio was a time when people _____.
   - Ⓐ watched TV shows
   - Ⓑ listened to radio shows
   - Ⓒ went to the movies
   - Ⓓ listened to a lot of songs

2. In the _____, there were no TVs and radio was new.
   - Ⓐ 1930s
   - Ⓑ 1940s
   - Ⓒ 1950s
   - Ⓓ 1960s

3. Soap operas began as radio shows. They got their name because _____.
   - Ⓐ the shows had a lot of soap in them
   - Ⓑ the shows were about washing with soap
   - Ⓒ the actors were doing an opera
   - Ⓓ soap makers put their ads on the shows

4. In a radio show, the actors _____.
   - Ⓐ wrote their own lines
   - Ⓑ made the sounds
   - Ⓒ read their lines into microphones
   - Ⓓ listened to the show

5. How were radio shows different from today's TV shows?
   - Ⓐ Radio shows had no actors.
   - Ⓑ Radio shows told stories.
   - Ⓒ Radio shows were only heard.
   - Ⓓ TV shows are live.

Bonus: On the back of this page, tell what you would like and what you would not like about listening to an old-time radio show.

Castles

Introducing the Topic

1. Reproduce page 159 for individual students, or make a transparency to use with a group or your whole class.

2. Present the castle diagram to students. Point out the castle's location. Discuss the location's advantages. Call attention to the different areas of the castle.

Reading the Selections

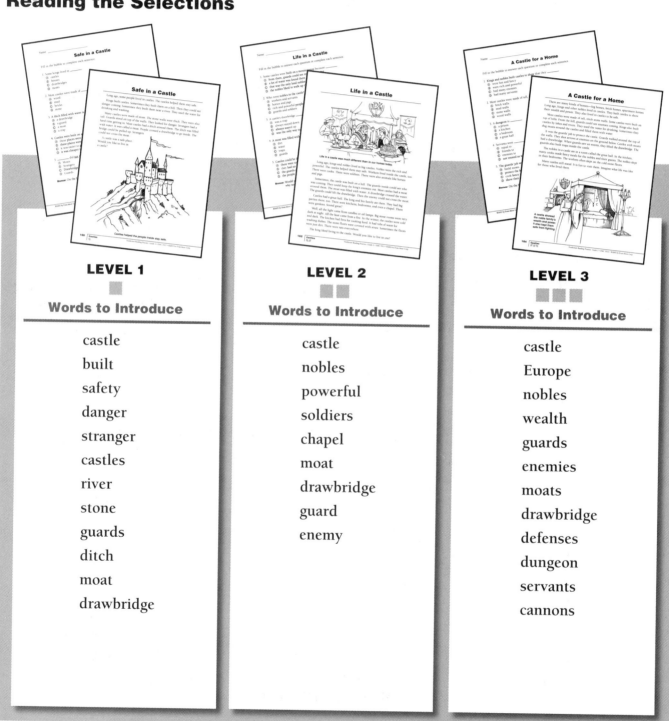

LEVEL 1
Words to Introduce

castle

built

safety

danger

stranger

castles

river

stone

guards

ditch

moat

drawbridge

LEVEL 2
Words to Introduce

castle

nobles

powerful

soldiers

chapel

moat

drawbridge

guard

enemy

LEVEL 3
Words to Introduce

castle

Europe

nobles

wealth

guards

enemies

moats

drawbridge

defenses

dungeon

servants

cannons

Nonfiction Reading Practice, Grade 2 • EMC 3313 • ©2003 by Evan-Moor Corp.

A Castle

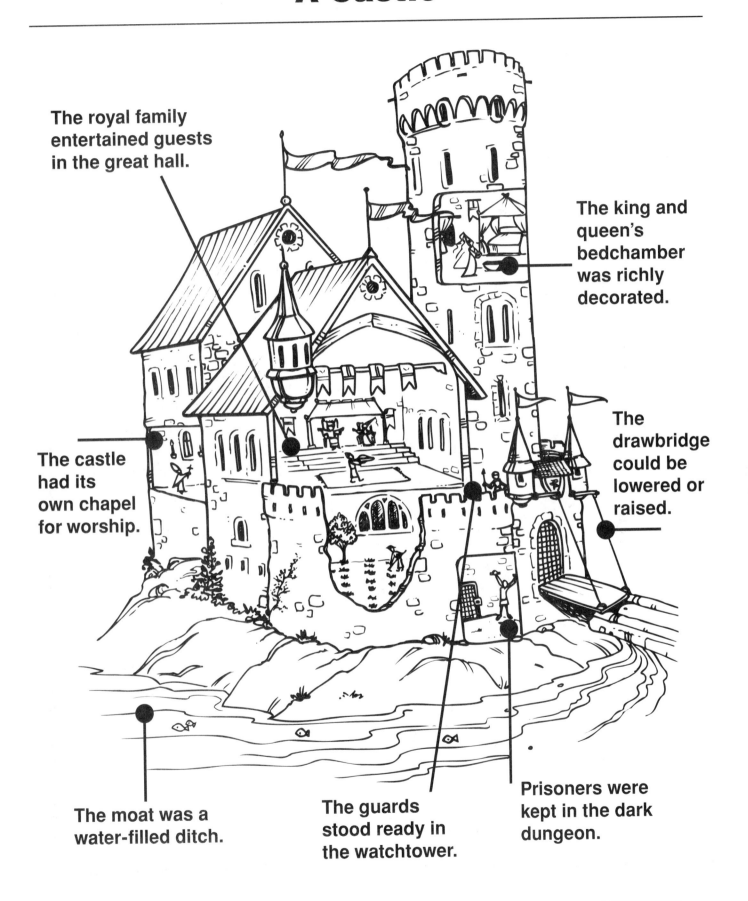

The royal family entertained guests in the great hall.

The king and queen's bedchamber was richly decorated.

The castle had its own chapel for worship.

The drawbridge could be lowered or raised.

The moat was a water-filled ditch.

The guards stood ready in the watchtower.

Prisoners were kept in the dark dungeon.

Safe in a Castle

Long ago, some people lived in castles. The castles helped them stay safe.

Kings built castles. Sometimes they built them on a hill. Then they could see danger coming. Sometimes they built them near a river. They used the water for drinking and washing.

Many castles were made of stone. The stone walls were thick. They were also tall. Guards stood on top of the walls. They looked for danger. Strangers had a hard time getting in. Most castles had a ditch around them. The ditch was filled with water. It was called a moat. People crossed a drawbridge to go inside. The bridge could be pulled up. Strangers could not cross the moat.

A castle was a safe place. Would you like to live in a castle?

Castles helped the people inside stay safe.

Nonfiction Reading Practice, Grade 2 • EMC 3313 • ©2003 by Evan-Moor Corp.

Name _____

Safe in a Castle

Fill in the bubble to complete each sentence.

1. Some kings lived in _____.
   - Ⓐ castles
   - Ⓑ houses
   - Ⓒ drawbridges
   - Ⓓ moats

2. Most castles were made of _____.
   - Ⓐ wood
   - Ⓑ mud
   - Ⓒ bricks
   - Ⓓ stone

3. A ditch filled with water is called _____.
   - Ⓐ a drawbridge
   - Ⓑ a guard
   - Ⓒ a moat
   - Ⓓ a trap

4. Castles were built on a hill because _____.
   - Ⓐ these places were safer than others
   - Ⓑ these places were prettier than others
   - Ⓒ it was easier to get water there
   - Ⓓ it was cheaper to build castles there

5. _____ did not protect the castle.
   - Ⓐ Moats
   - Ⓑ Strangers
   - Ⓒ Drawbridges
   - Ⓓ Guards

Bonus: On the back of this page, tell why a castle had a drawbridge.

Life in a Castle

Life in a castle was much different than in our homes today.

Long ago, kings and nobles lived in big castles. Nobles were the rich and powerful. The castles helped them stay safe. Workers lived inside the castle, too. There were cooks. There were soldiers. There were also animals like horses and pigs.

Sometimes, the castle was built on a hill. The guards inside could see who was coming. They could keep the king's enemies out. Most castles had a moat around them. The moat was filled with water. A drawbridge crossed the water. The guards could lift the drawbridge. Then the enemy could not cross the moat.

Castles had a great hall. The king and his family ate there. They had big parties there, too. There were kitchens, bedrooms, and even a chapel. There were gardens. Sound great?

Well, all the light came from candles or oil lamps. Big stone rooms were very dark at night. All the heat came from a fire. In the winter, the castles were cold and dark. The kitchen had fires for cooking food. It had tubs of water for washing dishes. The stone floors were covered with straw. Sometimes the floors were just dirt. There were rats everywhere.

The king liked living in the castle. Would you like to live in one?

Nonfiction Reading Practice, Grade 2 • EMC 3313 • ©2003 by Evan-Moor Corp.

Name _____

Life in a Castle

Fill in the bubble to answer each question or complete each sentence.

1. Some castles were built on a mountaintop because _____.
   - Ⓐ from there, guards could see enemies coming
   - Ⓑ a lot of water was found there
   - Ⓒ that was the only land nobles could use
   - Ⓓ the nobles liked to walk up the mountain

2. Who were **nobles** in the castle?
   - Ⓐ workers and servants
   - Ⓑ horses and pigs
   - Ⓒ rich and powerful people
   - Ⓓ guards and soldiers

3. A castle's drawbridge _____.
   - Ⓐ was a trap
   - Ⓑ always stayed down
   - Ⓒ always stayed up
   - Ⓓ was the only way to cross the moat

4. A moat was filled with _____.
   - Ⓐ dirt
   - Ⓑ water
   - Ⓒ traps
   - Ⓓ guards

5. Castles could be dark and cold because _____.
   - Ⓐ there were too many rooms in the castle
   - Ⓑ they had no lights and little heat in the castle
   - Ⓒ the guards could see enemies coming
   - Ⓓ the people who lived there could not pay for lights or heat

Bonus: Would you like to live in a castle? On the back of this page, tell why or why not.

A Castle for a Home

There are many kinds of homes—log homes, brick homes, apartment homes. Long ago, kings and other nobles lived in castles. They built castles to show their wealth and power. They also lived in castles to be safe.

Most castles were made of tall, thick stone walls. Some castles were built on top of hills. From the hill, guards could see enemies coming. Kings also built castles by lakes and rivers. They used the water for drinking. Sometimes they dug moats around the castles and filled them with water.

It was the guards' job to protect the castle. Guards walked around the top of the walls. They shot arrows at enemies on the ground below. Castles with moats had a drawbridge. When guards saw an enemy, they lifted the drawbridge. The guards also built traps inside the castle.

The nobles in a castle ate in a room called the great hall. In the kitchen, many cooks made fancy meals for the nobles and their guests. The nobles slept in their bedrooms. The workers often slept on the cold stone floors.

Many castles still stand. It is fun to visit them. Imagine what life was like for those who lived there.

A castle showed the noble family's wealth and power. It also kept them safe from fighting.

Nonfiction Reading Practice, Grade 2 • EMC 3313 • ©2003 by Evan-Moor Corp.

Name _____

A Castle for a Home

Fill in the bubble to answer each question or complete each sentence.

1. Kings and nobles built castles to show that they _____.
   - Ⓐ were fun and fancy
   - Ⓑ were rich and powerful
   - Ⓒ had many enemies
   - Ⓓ had many servants

2. Most castles were made of tall, thick _____.
   - Ⓐ brick walls
   - Ⓑ mud walls
   - Ⓒ stone walls
   - Ⓓ wood walls

3. A **dungeon** is _____.
   - Ⓐ a prison
   - Ⓑ a kitchen
   - Ⓒ a bedroom
   - Ⓓ a great hall

4. Servants were _____ the nobles.
   - Ⓐ equal to
   - Ⓑ friends to
   - Ⓒ enemies to
   - Ⓓ not treated as well as

5. The guards' job was to _____.
   - Ⓐ build moats
   - Ⓑ protect the king and nobles
   - Ⓒ cook fancy meals
   - Ⓓ show their power

Bonus: On the back of this page, tell what you learned about castles.

Name _____

A Famous Person

Write the important details about the famous person's life.

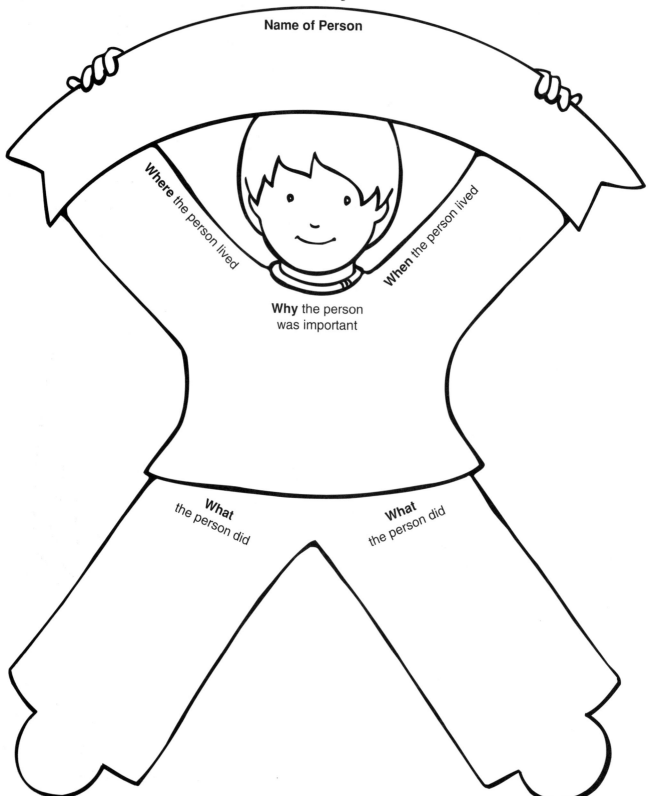

Name of Person

Where the person lived

When the person lived

Why the person
was important

What
the person did

What
the person did

Nonfiction Reading Practice, Grade 2 • EMC 3313 • ©2003 by Evan-Moor Corp.

Name _____

Fishbone Diagram

Write the main idea of the article on the fish's spine. Write the details between the other bones.

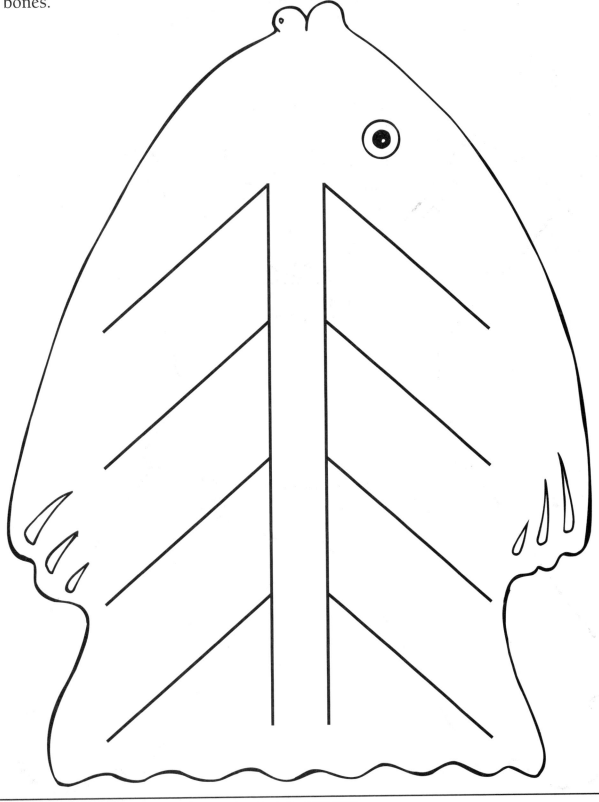

Name _____

Topic

_____

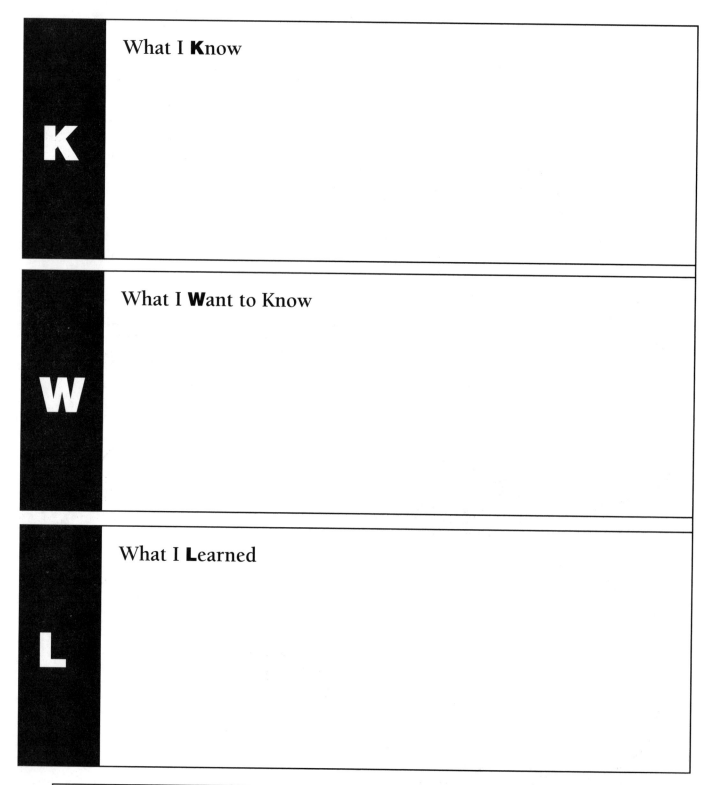

K   What I **K**now

W   What I **W**ant to Know

L   What I **L**earned

Name _____

Sequence Chart

Put the events of the article
in the correct order.

1

2

3

4

5

Name _____

Spider Web

Write the topic of the article in the center of the web. Write details about the topic in the sections of the web.

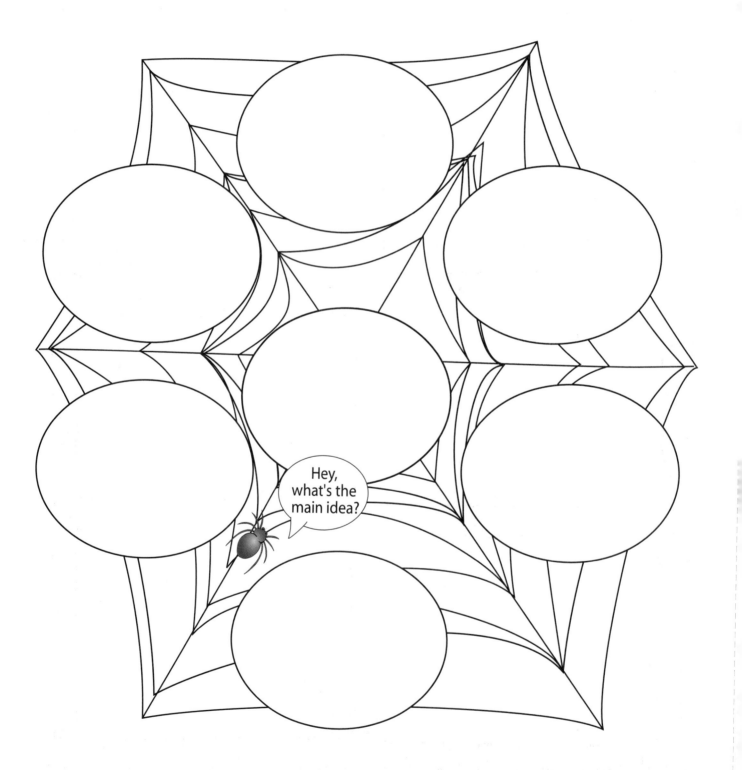

Nonfiction Reading Practice, Grade 2 • EMC 3313 • ©2003 by Evan-Moor Corp.

Name _____

Word Quilt

Write a new word you have learned in each quilt square. Write or draw what the word means in each quilt square.

Word: _____

Word: _____

Word: _____

Word: _____

Word: _____

Word: _____

Answer Key

page 9
1. C
2. A
3. B
4. C
5. D
Bonus: Answers will vary. Facts given might include: The Statue of Liberty is a famous statue. It is one of the tallest statues ever built. It is in New York Harbor. The Statue of Liberty is made of metal. She has a torch, a tablet, and a crown. She stands for freedom.

page 11
1. C
2. D
3. C
4. B
5. A
Bonus: Answers will vary, but might include: "Come in." "I'm glad you came." "It's nice to see you." "Thank you for coming." I could also smile, shake hands, or offer something to drink.

page 13
1. A
2. C
3. D
4. C
5. A
Bonus: Answers will vary. One interpretation could be: An invitation invites people to go somewhere or to do something. The Statue of Liberty stands in New York Harbor. She invites people to come to America to live and work.

page 17
1. C
2. A
3. A
4. B
5. D
Bonus: Answers will vary. A possible answer is: The president is the leader of America. He makes sure that people follow the laws of the country.

page 19
1. B
2. C
3. A
4. D
5. B
Bonus: Answers will vary. Students should relate facts about the president performing his many different roles well.

page 21
1. C
2. A
3. D
4. A
5. B
Bonus: Answers will vary. One interpretation could be: When a person becomes president, he makes a promise to the American people. He promises to defend the Constitution. He promises to be the chief executive, the leader of the armed forces, the foreign policy director, the legislative leader, and the chief of state.

page 25
1. A
2. B
3. D
4. B
5. D
Bonus: Answers will vary. Students should describe Harriet's decision to run away from her owners and return to the South to help other slaves run away.

page 27
1. A
2. B
3. D
4. B
5. C
Bonus: Answers will vary. One interpretation might be: Harriet Tubman was a hero because she helped other people even though it was dangerous. She worked to help slaves escape to the North, where they could be free.

page 29
1. C
2. C
3. D
4. A
5. D
Bonus: Answers will vary. A possible answer could be: Harriet Tubman had to be brave to run away from her owners. Then she made the dangerous trip many more times to help other slaves escape. It was dangerous, but she fought for liberty.

page 33
1. A
2. B
3. C
4. D
5. A

Bonus: Answers will vary. Facts given might include: In 1849, some people found gold in a river in California. Many other people went to California to find gold, too. They were excited about finding gold.

page 35
1. C
2. D
3. A
4. B
5. A

Bonus: Answers will vary, but should include an explanation for students' choices. One possible answer: If I lived in 1849, I would not go to California. I would not want to make the dangerous trip in a covered wagon. I might not even find gold. I would stay at my home.

page 37
1. D
2. A
3. A
4. B
5. C

Bonus: Answers will vary. One sample answer: I hit pay dirt! I came to California in a covered wagon. The trip was long and hard. The horses had a hard time climbing the mountains. I staked my claim on the American River. Right away, I found gold.

page 41
1. C
2. B
3. D
4. B
5. B

Bonus: H: Huron
O: Ontario
M: Michigan
E: Erie
S: Superior

page 43
1. D
2. A
3. C
4. D
5. B

Bonus: Answers will vary, but might include: I would see a lot of water and large ships carrying goods. I would probably see people having fun riding in boats and swimming in the water.

page 45
1. B
2. D
3. A
4. C
5. A

Bonus: Answers will vary. One correct response might be: Farmers and factory workers load their wheat and steel onto ships in the nearby lakes. The ships take the products to other places in the world. Since the Great Lakes are connected, the ships can sail from the factories to the Atlantic Ocean and then to any other place in the world.

page 49
1. B
2. A
3. B
4. D
5. C

Bonus: Answers will vary. Facts given might include: A magnet has a force that pulls metal things to itself. Magnets come in many shapes and sizes. All magnets have a north and south pole.

page 51
1. D
2. C
3. B
4. B
5. A

Bonus: Answers will vary. The list of magnetic objects should all be metal. The list of nonmagnetic objects should be made of various other materials.

page 53
1. D
2. A
3. C
4. A
5. B

Bonus: Answers will vary. Students should describe a working magnet trick from the article or one that the student creates.

page 57
1. B
2. C
3. C
4. A
5. B

Bonus: Answers will vary. Responses may include: Plants in a desert cannot grow close together. Some plants have long roots to get to the water in the ground. Other plants keep water in their roots, stems, and leaves.

page 59
1. B
2. C
3. B
4. D
5. B

Bonus: Answers will vary, but might include: Many different animals live in the desert. Most of them hide during the day because it is too hot. They stay in burrows, then come out at night to eat.

page 61
1. A
2. C
3. B
4. B
5. C

Bonus: Answers will vary. An explanation could include: A mesquite tree has very long roots to get water that's deep in the ground. The barrel cactus keeps water in its stem. It uses the water until it rains again. It also has sharp spines to keep animals from getting the water in its stem.

page 65
1. D
2. A
3. B
4. A
5. C

Bonus: Students' drawings and labels should include a new moon, a crescent moon, a quarter moon, and a full moon.

page 67
1. C
2. B
3. B
4. A
5. D

Bonus: Answers will vary. A possible answer could be: The light from the flashlight stands for the sun. The foam ball moves around the globe. Even though the flashlight is always shining on the foam ball, the light shines on different places. The light shows us the phases of the moon we see from Earth.

page 69
1. C
2. A
3. C
4. B
5. A

Bonus: Answers will vary. One comparison could be: In a solar eclipse, the moon is between the sun and Earth. The moon hides the sun. In a lunar eclipse, Earth is between the sun and the moon. Earth blocks the sun's light. The moon looks red.

page 73
1. B
2. A
3. C
4. D
5. B

Bonus: Answers will vary. Explanations may include: The Hubble space telescope takes pictures of things that are very far away. We learn about things in space when we look at the pictures.

page 75
1. C
2. B
3. B
4. A
5. D

Bonus: Answers will vary, but might include: Astronomers on the ground use computers. The computers can tell the Hubble space telescope what to look at and what to take pictures of.

page 77
1. A
2. B
3. C
4. D
5. A

Bonus: Answers will vary. One interpretation could be: The Hubble space telescope has found and taken pictures of things in space that we did not know were there.

page 81
1. B
2. D
3. C
4. D
5. A

Bonus: Answers will vary. Explanations may include: Lightning hit the metal on the kite. Then it went down the string and hit the key. It made a spark.

page 83
1. C
2. B
3. A
4. D
5. B

Bonus: Answers will vary, but might include: The Gulf Stream is like a river under the water. It pushes boats along.

page 85
1. C
2. B
3. C
4. B
5. A

Bonus: Answers will vary. Students should name an invention and tell what it does.

page 89
1. B
2. D
3. D
4. C
5. C
Bonus: Students' answers should contain the name of an exercise and describe its benefits, such as developing a stronger heart and body.

page 91
1. C
2. D
3. A
4. B
5. B
Bonus: Answers will vary. Students should identify three aerobic activities that can be done independently, three aerobic activities that can be done with a group, and their favorite activity.

page 93
1. D
2. B
3. C
4. B
5. A
Bonus: Answers will vary. One interpretation could be: People who say, "No pain, no gain," mean that exercise has to hurt to make your muscles stronger. Exercise should be fun and pain free. It should not hurt.

page 97
1. C
2. A
3. D
4. C
5. A
Bonus: Answers will vary, but may include such things as bones, toys, cars, or furniture.

page 99
1. B
2. C
3. B
4. D
5. C
Bonus: Answers will vary. Students should reference a broken bone on a leg, arm, finger, or other body part.

page 101
1. C
2. D
3. B
4. B
5. C

Bonus: Students' answers should reference hairline, complete, greenstick, and open fractures.

page 105
1. D
2. A
3. C
4. B
5. A
Bonus: Answers will vary. One reason could be: Clara Barton cared about the hurt soldiers. She cooked for them, stayed with them, talked to them, and listened to them.

page 107
1. A
2. B
3. A
4. C
5. D
Bonus: Answers will vary. Students should identify a Red Cross effort either from the article or the news.

page 109
1. D
2. A
3. D
4. B
5. C
Bonus: Answers will vary. One interpretation could be: Clara Barton went to the hurt soldiers in the battlefield. She stayed with them, talked to them, and listened to them. She made them feel better.

page 113
1. D
2. B
3. A
4. C
5. B
Bonus: Answers will vary. Students should identify an item, its approximate cost, and the amount needed to purchase the item.

page 115
1. B
2. C
3. A
4. D
5. B
Bonus: Answers will vary, but might include: To be a smart shopper, think about what you want to buy. You should also round the prices to the nearest dollar and add them in your head. You need to keep track of your total cost.

page 117
1. A
2. B
3. A
4. B
5. D

Bonus: Answers will vary. One explanation could be: When the price of something ends with more than 50¢, you round up to the nearest dollar. Milk costs $1.89. The price ends with more than 50¢. You can say that the milk costs about $2.00.

page 121
1. B
2. C
3. A
4. C
5. D

Bonus: Answers will vary. Students should identify a fraction from the recipe and show how it is used. For example, students could identify 1/2 of a lime and draw a picture showing a lime cut in half with one half circled.

page 123
1. A
2. C
3. B
4. B
5. A

Bonus: Answers will vary. Students should write a fraction using cookie numbers and identify its meaning. For example, 2/5 means two of five equal parts.

page 125
1. B
2. A
3. D
4. C
5. B

Bonus: Answers will vary. Students should identify two fractions from the recipe, such as 1/3 and 1/4. They should then give pictorial representations of the fractions, such as a circle divided into three equal parts with one part shaded, and a circle divided into four equal parts with one part shaded.

page 129
1. A
2. A
3. B
4. C
5. D

Bonus: Answers will vary. One possibility is: Measure a pencil with centimeters and a house with meters.

page 131
1. B
2. A
3. D
4. B
5. B

Bonus: Answers will vary, but might include: Millimeters and centimeters are too small to measure a room. You would have to count too many lines on the ruler. Use meters because they are bigger than millimeters and centimeters.

page 133
1. D
2. B
3. B
4. A
5. C

Bonus: Answers will vary. One possibility is: You would measure with meters if you were measuring a person. You would measure with kilometers if you were measuring the distance from one town to another. Measure an ant with millimeters and a pencil with centimeters.

page 137
1. B
2. C
3. C
4. D
5. D

Bonus: Answers will vary. Examples of things to sing about might be: family, friends, pets, or the environment.

page 139
1. B
2. C
3. B
4. A
5. D

Bonus: Answers will vary. An example might be: "Whistle While You Work."

page 141
1. B
2. D
3. A
4. D
5. C

Bonus: Answers will vary. One response could be: singing together helped the sailors work together. Singing helped pass the time away.

Nonfiction Reading Practice, Grade 2 • EMC 3313 • ©2003 by Evan-Moor Corp.